The Psychologist & Her Narcissists

A Guide to Surviving Toxic Relationships

Jenny Tamasi

LIONWOOD
PUBLISHING

A Lala Media Company
LionWood Publishing

First published in Great Britain in 2020 by Lionwood Publishing.
www.lionwoodpublishing.com

hello@lionwoodpublishing.com
@lionwoodpublishing

This edition published in 2020

ISBN 978-1-8381930-0-3

Printed and bound in Great Britain.

The Psychologist &
Her Narcissists

Contents

To all the survivors of toxic and dysfunctional relationships, your stories and experiences are courageous and important. I believe you.

Authors Note

Thank you for reading my book.

Writing this book has been a very therapeutic and educational process for me and I hope that you are also able to learn and benefit from my experiences and research.

I wish you well on your healing journey.

I would like to thank my support system for listening, visiting, calling, taking me on holidays, bringing me ice-cream, going for walks, and always being there for me.

I am so lucky to have you in my life.

I love you!

I would also like to express my gratitude and appreciation to my editor and publishing company who have been very patient and helpful during the development of this book.

Disclaimer

The purpose of this book is to provide education and general information that is in the interest of the public. While the advice is written from the perspective, knowledge base, and opinions of a mental health professional, the author is not directly treating or counselling her readers and is not responsible for their care. Readers should consult with their mental health care provider for guidance about their treatment and diagnostics.

In the case of a mental health crisis or other emergencies, seek emergency medical services or contact your local police. References are provided for informational purposes only and do not reflect any specific endorsements.

The names, settings, descriptions, and other identifying information of the people in the case studies in this book have been changed to protect their privacy and anonymity. Any resemblance to any actual persons is purely coincidental. The events, conversations, and information published in this book are based on the truth, the author's recollection of the events described, and her memories of the individuals in the case studies and how they presented.

For this book, some events have been compressed and do not follow a chronological timeline. As we know in psychology, memories are imperfect, and the examples documented in this book are the author's interpretation and opinions of issues related to relationships. Specific examples were used to highlight and to educate readers about commonalities in these types of relationships. The author did not include these examples with the intent to embarrass or to cause any hardships for the individuals in the case studies.

The author has forgiven these individuals and wishes them well.

PART 1

"Love felt by the parent does not automatically translate into love experienced by the child."

—GABOR MATE

Prologue

I am a psychologist and I work with children and adults. The title of this book comes from two very dysfunctional relationships that I had with men, both of whom demonstrated personality traits associated with disturbing or difficult personalities. As a mental health professional, I would say they fall under the umbrella of characteristics commonly observed in Cluster B personality disorders.

The Diagnostic and Statistical Manual of Mental Disorders "DSM-5" shows that there are many similarities between the criteria for Borderline Personality Disorder, Narcissistic Personality Disorder, Histrionic Personality Disorder, and Antisocial Personality Disorder. These are what we refer to as the Cluster B Personality Disorders. For this book, I am going to refer to the negative effects of being in a relationship with an individual with Cluster B personality traits as narcissistic abuse. I'm also going to refer to my ex-lovers as narcissists. This is just semantics to keep things straight, I am not formally diagnosing either of them, just describing my observations using my knowledge of these disorders and the symptoms that they presented.

Cluster B Personality Types

Diagnosing a personality disorder can be tricky due to the overlap of symptoms. I like to think of mental health conditions as a spectrum of symptoms and traits to guide treatment, and in my opinion, sometimes the diagnosis isn't the most important thing to nail down.

We are all on the mental health spectrum somewhere. Thankfully we do not all have personality disorders, but I don't believe there are many individuals who do not need to work on and improve their mental health. If you are learning about Cluster B Personality Disorders or narcissists for the first time, then please remember that nobody meets every single diagnostic criterion and they don't have to for a diagnosis. Even if a person only has a few traits, they could still be highly toxic in a relationship of any sort.

What are narcissistic traits, I hear you thinking? The most common ones are a sense of superiority, entitlement, self-importance, self-centeredness, arrogance, grandiosity, lack of empathy, excessive need for affirmation, manipulative and selfish would all classify as a very good start.

Unfortunately, in the world we live in today with social media, reality TV and dysfunctional family structures now generational in much of the world, these may all sound like common traits that many people you know display. The difference between a narcissist or someone a little full of themselves is the extreme to which people who have personality disorders will display these traits. Usually, the closest family members or intimate partners are the ones who get to experience this side of the narcissist's character. In other settings, the same person may behave in a charismatic and helpful, generous and honest or even very humble way; we call this the representative, and we will talk more about this later on in the book.

The Narcissistic Lover

This book is all about being in relationships with a narcissist; well two of them to be precise, one after the other. You may be wondering how that happened to a smart, educated woman like me? At the beginning of both relationships, all I saw was this ideal individual that the narcissist portrays to others, and I believed it, both times. Once the narcissist is in an intimate relationship, due to the dynamics and demands of such, the narcissist can't keep their nicer than nice image going forever.

Whether it takes a few months or years for the representative to leave, every narcissist eventually shows their real traits. Throughout the book, I will refer to commonly used phrases that are related to narcissistic abuse such as; love-bombing, gaslighting, and future-faking. You may or may not be familiar with some of the terms I use, so I'll give a clear definition - with examples from my own experiences as they come up in the book.

If you are dating, married to or have an ex that you suspect is a narcissist, I'm sure you will find many of the stories fascinating and inspirational. If this is all new to you, then I'm sure you'll find some of these stories eye-opening and perhaps even quite alarming. Many of you reading this book may have a friend or family member who appears to be in a relationship with someone who seems to fit the traits of a narcissist - if this is the case, then recommend they read this book and make up their mind - it's the only way to effect change.

Speaking of change, that is the reasoning behind me laying my life onto the pages that follow in this book. My experiences caused a tremendous amount of change in my life, some good and some bad. While I do not profess to be able to save everyone from having a narcissistic relationship, I hope that by reading this book you will be able to take my stories, the red flags and reflections that I share so that you can make the change that improves your life.

If you are reading this book to learn about the narcissistic traits or behaviours of your romantic partner, then I would suggest focusing on how their personality traits negatively impact the lives of others, and of course *you*. Then decide on how you plan to process the experience and heal. This book is not about them; it's about you, your life and your recovery!

Also, by taking the time to recognise and understand these traits and characteristics, you will better identify them when they show up in people that you meet in the future. While you may find yourself asking, "Why would they do this to me?" or, "What did I do to cause this?" it's not necessarily the best use of your time or energy. The truth is usually quite simple and is typically related to the fact that they are narcissists and very toxic people. When you can accept that it is okay to not know the "why " or the "how" of your abuser, you can begin to explore the "why" and the "how" of your own behaviours and feelings so you can start the healing process and avoid the same painful mistakes in the future.

Now, as a mental health professional, you may be wondering if I feel empathy or sorrow for my ex-lovers because they probably have severe psychological disorders and multiple diagnosable mental health conditions. That is a tricky question to answer. I am going to answer it as the ex-girlfriend first because that is who I am to them, and not as a therapist. Narcissists know right from wrong and understand social rules and norms, but they decide not to follow them. Sometimes when I think how empty they are on the inside or how they are not able to feel emotions the way we can, I feel sad for them. I would never want their lives or to treat others how they do. Sometimes I feel embarrassed for them. However, while I recognise that their feelings, behaviours and thought processes are abnormal, I no longer excuse these things or want someone who hurts me in my life.

Now, as a therapist, I would say, I have compassion for myself first and foremost. If another person's mental health is negatively impacting your life, in any way, it's okay to protect yourself and remove that person from your life. Always create boundaries that will keep you safe. Remember it isn't your job to treat or cure your partner in a romantic relationship. Staying away from someone with psychological problems who hurts you is a smart thing to do; this is no cause for shame or guilt. While we can't always choose who the members of our family are, and we may have to tolerate individuals with personality disorders or mental health conditions in our personal lives, we can choose who our romantic partners are. Choose wisely.

Red Flags

Red flags are signs; sometimes subtle, other times more obvious. They can be intuitive, or practical, and show up in all areas of life; anything from buying a car to starting a new job. Red flags will usually give you a weird feeling in your stomach or make you pause and think. Red flags can be a feeling that something is off, or a huge flashing neon sign that it's time to turn and run.

In this book, red flags for me were all of the signs that I wasn't being treated well, and that something was wrong with my relationship. I often missed my red flags and only saw them in the rearview mirror once I started the process of healing and doing my internal work.

I discovered that once I had recovered from narcissistic abuse, red flags became deal breakers for me. As you recover, it is likely that you will begin to have stronger reactions to red flags and this is a good sign!

Often because of conditioning from childhood, we accept or ignore bad behaviours or things that make us feel uncomfortable on the inside. As a result, we learn to ignore our intuition and instincts and hope for the best instead of resolving concerns in relationships. In my case as a little girl, my parents always told me that children were not allowed to be angry. If I did not like a rule or a punishment, too bad. They also followed that old school philosophy of children should be seen and not heard. My expressions of sadness, injustice, anger, or any negativity at home were not welcomed.

Both of my parents were screamers and I learned from an early age that their anger would eventually pass and they would be my loving parents again soon. In my subconscious, I internalised the message that people who love you and keep you safe sometimes lash out at you or yell at you for no good reason and you need to accept that as part of the relationship. So since I was also taught that being angry or complaining as a child was wrong, I ignored behaviours that were upsetting to me and pushed my feelings away as an adult too.

Red flags are important to pay attention to because they are the building blocks to toxic patterns in relationships. *In relationships, it is crucial to pay attention to actions and words, not just words.* Sadly, lies, insults, disappearing acts, anger outbursts, selfish behaviour, and cheating turn into repeated offences that tend to become ongoing patterns in relationships. When you are in love, especially in the beginning stages, you do not want to think that your new partner has a tragic flaw or is bad for you. *It is easy to avoid the red flags to keep the excitement and ideal image of your partner intact.* If you are guilty of this, join the club! It is easy to do and you can learn from it in the future. Forgive yourself for missing the red flags.

Paying attention to red flags can be scary because once we recognise a problem we have to do something about it. Once we identify a red flag, it prompts actions, and tough conversations can be scary. It is normal to feel anxious and uncomfortable when we identify red flags and have to make decisions about them. I would encourage you to not be afraid to let go of things that are not good for you. If something doesn't feel right, and especially if this becomes a pattern, step away.

So to sum it up, red flags are things that signal something is wrong that you need to address and pay attention to in your life, and especially in your relationships.

If you notice inconsistencies or traits that just do not feel right, pay attention to your gut. Do not avoid confrontations or tough conversations because you do not want to make waves or make someone feel upset. A healthy partner can handle questions about their actions and why they did or did not do or say something.

I use red flags as a teaching tool in this book because I wish I would have paid attention to them in my two toxic relationships; it would have saved me so much time and pain. I always tried to help, heal, and change my partners and hoped that the red flags would go away or at least get fixed. They never got fixed or improved, and they certainly didn't disappear.

If you are in a relationship with a narcissist, the red flags will turn into patterns that will hurt you. A narcissist may promise to fix or change their behaviour but they rarely do. They promise to change to manipulate you and to keep you around. You do not need to give people second or third chances and once you observe the red flags of narcissism or dysfunctional relationships, it is much better to cut your losses and get out.

Chapter 1

I Forgive You - Mum & Dad

TRAUMA IS A HUMAN condition. Whether we realise it or not, our childhood and our relationships with our primary caregivers have a significant impact on who we are in relationships as adults. For most of us, our parents provided the framework for our concepts of romantic relationships; what we consider to be "normal" or tolerable often comes from what we saw as children at home. It's also not unusual for us to subconsciously choose a romantic partner that reminds us of one of our parents. If you have been in therapy before, you know that sooner or later you will talk about your family of origin and make connections between your childhood and your adult life. If you make a list of your mother and father's personality traits and the traits of your previous partners, you probably will see similarities.

In my case, I had two parents who loved me very much and tried their best to raise healthy children. While I give them a great deal of credit for all of their good intentions and efforts, they are both human and therefore have their faults.

When I first started processing my romantic relationships, it was difficult for me to see my mother in my first narcissistic lover. It took about a year in therapy for me to make that connection because I love my mother, and she has contributed to many of my strengths as a woman and adult. It was hard to accept that, unintentionally, my mother contributed to my patterns and pathology, creating many of my most significant flaws as an adult. I always thought I saw so much of my father in my second selfish lover, and when his secrets were revealed, it was extremely disappointing to realise how wrong I was.

Seeing your parents as people who have damaged you can be painful and challenging to process, but it is possible. *Analysing your childhood is a good place to begin your healing journey.* If you have childhood wounds that haven't been dealt with, they will show up in some way. These wounds need to be understood and healed to avoid unhealthy patterns as an adult. I had no clue I even had childhood wounds or that my relationships followed a pattern until I was in therapy.

As a child, I wanted attention and approval from my parents more than anything, and also to avoid conflicts. This desire turned me into a "people-pleaser" and someone willing to work very hard to make others happy. My home environment also created a person who had a high tolerance for abuse. Even though I took countless courses in psychology in graduate school, I never made this connection. I needed a therapist to point out this connection, and guide me through the understanding of the "why" I did things and "where" my behaviours were formed. It's easy to remain blinded by false perceptions or nostalgia if you don't take the time to think about and dissect your past.

My Mother and Narcissist Number One

My mother was a screamer; she would scream first and think later. My father was very anxious and overprotective. He always thought I was at risk of dying or being in a tragic accident. My parents thought instilling fear in their children was instilling respect in them and would ultimately keep them safe. I hated being yelled at over what I considered "small stuff" so as a child, my response to perceived danger or fear was to freeze.

Although she didn't realise this, *my mother's harsh communication style conditioned me to dissociate when something was threatening or wrong in my adult relationships.* My dad's nervousness around perceived dangers made me fearful and reinforced my freezing behaviour. I figured out that due to my childhood and the traumatic experiences of being yelled at and smothered, *I often overlooked red flags and any inappropriate behaviour in romantic relationships.* I put this down to my not learning how to recognise and manage any indiscretions, as I had an inbuilt fear of challenging, and due to being overly protected as a child or young person, I very rarely had to react to or take action in response to red flags.

When my first narcissist would explode over dinner being late or me not ironing a shirt up to his standards, I subconsciously reverted to the defence mechanism I used when I was a little girl - I would freeze, not dare to talk back, and apologise. I would get yelled at frequently for not doing household chores well enough as a kid so it was easy to accept this and fall back into that pattern of being yelled at by someone I loved. This was a behaviour I practised so much as a child as I learned that it helped to keep the situation stable and not make it worse. Freezing and apologising when I'd done nothing wrong then became ingrained in me as the automatic coping mechanisms that I used as an adult. Unfortunately, because screaming and insults were common in my childhood home, I didn't think they were abnormal to experience in a romantic relationship.

I also had a deep desire to please others, whether my parents or partners, and as a result, I would avoid doing anything that might disappoint my partners. I also had a high tolerance for feeling afraid, or anxious and had become an overachiever, not wanting to fail or risk losing love. I was also used to yelling and bickering at home and I assumed that was what relationships eventually turned into. I also was always anticipating the fear and confrontation that I now believed as a result of my childhood, were typical parts of everyday life.

My Father and Narcissist Number Two

Moving on to adult life, after leaving my first narcissist, who had an exaggerated and much more intense version of my mother's personality traits, I desperately wanted to be with the opposite of that overt, explosive and difficult lover. Subconsciously, I looked for my father. *My dad is known as a nice guy who would do anything for anyone,* who likes to work with his hands and fix things, and *who spoils my mother and probably has some codependent traits.* I have much more of my dad's personality traits than my mom's. So, only weeks after I moved out of my home with number one I met number two. Physically and personality-wise, he reminded me of my dad. Therefore I thought he was "safe," and I was hoping he would take care of me and commit to me as my father did with my mother. I thought he did, but as you read you will discover how I really called that one wrong!

I have learned to take a balanced approach to analyse the good and the bad when considering childhood trauma, my family of origin and upbringing. My understanding is there is good and bad in every family. I guess what I am trying to say is that we all have issues that stem from our upbringing, and once we become aware of these it really helps when figuring out how we managed to get into a toxic relationship, but more importantly what we need to work on to get out of one.

Red Flags

Red flags for childhood trauma that could lead to avoiding red flags as an adult:

- Your parents' moods were very up and down and you didn't know why

- Your parents applied inconsistent punishments, often surprising you

- Your parents used very harsh punishments to teach you lessons

- Your parents taught you that fear is respect

- Your parents screamed at you for little things like not cleaning the bathroom with the right cleaner, not having nice penmanship, or leaving your jacket on a chair

- Your parents did not validate your emotions or feelings

- Your parents expected you to take care of their emotional needs

- Your parents placed responsibility on you for adult stuff like taking care of the house, relationships and bills.

- Your parents blamed you for their emotions

- Your parents never said thank you, please or apologised to you

- Your parents did not comfort you when you were sad or recognise when you were angry

- Your parents had unrealistic or extremely high expectations for you academically, in sports, and for your future

Before you move on to the next chapter, spend 15 - 20 minutes reflecting on what you have read, using the points below.

- Reflect on the positive and negative personality traits you see in your childhood caregivers and in your abusive partner. Do you see similarities? If it helps, write them down in a journal or use the notes at the end of the book.

- Reflecting on your childhood wounds is something you can do on a regular basis - these tend to show up like an onion, each layer you peel away could bring tears.

- How would you describe your relationship with each parent? Whatever it was, be honest with yourself and it will become easier to connect the dots with your current relationship.

- What trauma have you experienced in childhood, no matter how seemingly small or insignificant, that you haven't dealt with?

- What do you need to forgive yourself or a parent for?

- Where can you see a connection in the way you were raised that shows up in your tolerance for unhealthy or inappropriate behaviour?

- List the personality traits you have that you are most proud of. What are the personality traits that you would like to modify or that have been problematic for you in relationships?

Chapter 2

Stella Artois!

HE LITERALLY HAD ME at hello! Miguel was a handsome and charismatic doctor from Portugal who was completing his residency at the hospital where my mother worked as a nurse. I met him because he was my grandmother's doctor, and my aunt and mother introduced us. Both my aunt and mother are very smart and educated women and they thought that Miguel was the greatest, most charming guy they had ever met. I also remember telling my mother and aunt that I did not want to call or contact my grandmother's doctor, as I thought this was weird and unethical. My mother and my aunt both really encouraged me and frequently asked when I was going to call the handsome young resident. Me, in my typical people-pleaser fashion, decided that sending a quick text message would satisfy my family, then I could say I did as I was told. In that message I thanked Miguel for being kind to my grandmother, then he called me, and that is how the relationship began.

Miguel looked great on paper; he was an educated, handsome, charming doctor that my family loved. I love meeting people from different cultures and Miguel seemed to not only fit the bill but was like a dream come true. I also loved the attention and how he made me feel in the beginning; so much so that I began to really minimise and forget about my needs and feelings.

Now, obviously, everyone's perception of Miguel has changed completely; but at the beginning of our relationship, Miguel was extremely affectionate and charming, but that soon changed. All of my family really liked him and enjoyed spending time with him. While it appeared that Miguel had nothing in common with any of my middle-class conservative family members, somehow he fit right in. They all loved him! He could win almost anyone over and even though English wasn't his first language he had a knack with anecdotes and local phrases.

Miguel was an extreme thinker, like my mother, and would explode, becoming verbally aggressive over little things such as not cutting the vegetables up small enough, putting too many meatballs in the frying pan at one time, or kissing him on the cheek in public and not on the lips. With Miguel, I constantly felt like I was walking on eggshells because I never knew what would set him off.

Miguel was also very controlling and liked to tell me how to dress, talk, and who I should be friends with. When Miguel came home from work the expectation was that my hair was done, earrings in, my makeup was freshly applied and I would be wearing a dress and heels or some other approved outfit. My mother also still tries to advise me on what I should wear and what I should say in social situations but in a much milder way. Miguel did this just to be controlling and always wanted things his way. He simply could not tolerate anyone contradicting him or disagreeing with him. If I ever did, he would scream at me in public or at home.

For example, a few of Miguel's doctor friends were visiting us for a weekend and somehow the subject of piercing a baby girl's ears came up. I didn't understand at the time what a loaded or hot button issue, this would be for him. I remember casually saying that if I had a daughter, that I would not pierce her ears as an infant, that I didn't agree with it and didn't like how it looked on little babies. I didn't really think anything of my comment; I was just stating my opinion and participating in the conversation. Miguel became so upset that he went upstairs to bed and left his friends with me in the living room. He also refused to talk to any of us the next day and refused to take his friends back to the train station because I disagreed with him in front of his peers. The 24 hours that followed the earring discussion were extremely tense and Miguel shifted between glaring at me and avoiding me every chance he could. His friends were extremely uncomfortable and I was mortified.

Typically after one of his rages, I would get the silent treatment and end up apologising so that his angry glares would stop. Miguel would also blame me for making him so angry that he had to act like a toddler. His behaviour was always my fault in his mind. Miguel liked to remind me that he was smarter than me, that he had dated girls who were prettier than me and that I really was not all that special. It was no secret that Miguel liked women: he would openly tell me that he looked at pornography, he would flirt with girls in front of me and he would compare me to previous girlfriends. What did I do when he told me those things? Usually, I would freeze and say nothing, sometimes I would change the subject and sometimes I would laugh it off. Did I ever stand up for myself or say that I didn't like his open love for women? Rarely, if ever.

Miguel also loved himself more than anything. He loved to groom himself, take care of himself and buy himself presents. Miguel always took longer to get ready than I did. The expectation was that I would always look impeccable, always be happy, and always cater to his needs. I was never allowed to have a ponytail and pyjama day at home. Miguel was a flashy dresser who liked brand names. Of course, the expectation was that I would also always wear designer labels.

I remember one day, Miguel and I went shopping at a luxury designer store, at his request. Miguel held up a purple leather handbag that he wanted me to buy for myself. It was very well-made and elegant to look at; when I asked about the price, the sales assistant informed me that the bag cost £3,500. I told her that the bag was beautiful; and gave it back. There was no way that I could afford to pay that and I also think that is too much money to splurge on a handbag. In usual Miguel fashion, he stormed out of the store saying how I had embarrassed him because I was being cheap. I chased after him and said I was sorry. For what, I really didn't even know at the time, but we were in public and people were looking at him and I just wanted the show to stop.

Maybe you are asking yourself what the heck did you stick around for? I stuck around for the same reason that people who win big for the first time, return to the casino. The initial love-bombing I experienced with Miguel, followed by intermittent reinforcement such as, over the top apologies and grand gestures when he did something that was really bad or upsetting to me.

While Miguel rarely apologised, when he did decide to apologise he did it very well, and usually, the really big explosions were followed by passionate makeup sex. When he would have an explosion sometimes he would buy me a present or take me somewhere that I liked, and of course, he was very nice for a few days. The truth is, these are the things that kept me going in the relationship.

This cycle in relationships is what gets us hooked; it's a pattern that is typical of forming a trauma bond. *A trauma bond is the result of the cycle of attention and love mixed with abuse and punishment that repeats over time, creating a form of codependency and very powerful attachments.*

Initially, whenever Miguel would have an "episode" of blind anger, intense rage, or was just downright mean, it seemed so out of character. Then the kind and sweet, successful boyfriend would come back and act as if nothing had happened. As the years passed I saw the explosive and entitled guy way more than the nice, sweet guy. The fact that the "good Miguel" showed up every now and then made me hopeful that he would come back for good and stay.

Instead of seeing the red flags for what they were, signs to head for the hills, I rationalised and made excuses for his behaviour. This was easy to do because he played the victim role so well. I thought Miguel's bad behaviour had to be the result of working such long hours in the hospital, cultural differences, and stress. I thought that after his residency things would get better - instead they just got worse. I thought that after he got accustomed to being a surgeon, things would improve, but they became significantly worse. His behaviour simply got worse.

Eventually, Miguel's tantrums, dirty looks, flirting with other women, and other overtly disrespectful behaviours became obvious to my friends and family. I would either make excuses for him or defend him. Had I acknowledged what actually was going on, I would have had to do something about it. I had become addicted to this relationship and clung to the highs and dissociated from the lows.

The fact that Miguel was a very difficult person was no secret to me and over time it became clear to the people in my world. During one of our first phone conversations, I remember him telling me he was a very complicated person. I remember thinking that was an odd thing to say, but I brushed it off. Miguel's overt narcissism was subtle at first, but it was definitely there and over time, it became more and more obvious. The lesson here? When people show or tell you who they are, believe them.

Even though eventually Miguel wore his narcissism on his sleeve, he did have a sneaky side. I am sure there are many things he did without me knowing, but during the fifth year of our relationship, one day I was unpacking his suitcase following his return from a trip to visit his family. (I was never invited on these family trips). During the unpacking, I noticed a page of his passport had a pink stamp on it. I'm not a natural snooper and would usually be afraid to go through his things. Who knows, maybe subconsciously I was always afraid of what I might find, and I was certainly afraid of the punishment I would receive if I got caught. Nevertheless that day I opened up his passport and found stamps for France, Germany and Luxembourg. Miguel wasn't visiting his family that he claimed to miss so dearly; he had been living a double life.

After finding his passport, I experienced my own rage. I called him and confronted him. I felt panicked, anxious, angry, and confused. I normally would never talk to Miguel in this tone but I felt so upset. What the heck was he doing in all these places? Why was he lying to me? Miguel told me to go to the shop and buy him a six-pack of Stella Artois - his preferred lager - otherwise, he was not going to come home and tell me what was going on. I gathered my composure and like the obedient girlfriend that I was, I went to the corner shop and bought the lager. That night, Miguel came home and told me that he had impregnated a girl in France.

As you can imagine after cooking, cleaning, running errands and correcting grammar mistakes on countless presentations for five years, this news hit me like a ton of bricks. Of course, Miguel cried and showed fake remorse. He never left our home or left my side, all the time, implying that his French girlfriend and child would, in fact, be living in the UK. At the breaking point, I decided to leave him. Although the only reason I actually left was that I could not stand the thought of him replacing me and leaving me, it was over nevertheless.

That was my first move towards keeping some of my dignity. So, I impulsively bought a house close to my work, packed up and left. I told my friends and family after the dust had settled. I kept my move and the unborn child a secret as long as I could because I just felt so embarrassed. My life was looking like Eastenders or some other soap opera.

Miguel's Red Flags

Miguel's signs of overt personality traits that were red flags that I ignored:

- Sense of entitlement
- Always needing to have things his way
- Overreacting to criticism
- Talking and boasting excessively about his accomplishments
- Prioritising image and superficial things to the extreme
- Emotionally needy
- Insulting to me, my friends, and my family
- Cheating
- Very high sex drive, obsession with sex
- Needing a lot of attention and affection
- Lying
- Exaggerating
- Inability to handle rejection, criticism or other opinions
- Talking about other women and pornography openly
- Impulsive

- Putting himself and his needs first, always
- Extremely competitive
- Tantrums
- Controlling my image, behaviours and relationships
- Lack of remorse
- Superficial charm
- Extremely charismatic
- Risk-taking behaviour: reckless driving, unprotected sex.

Reflecting on that list of red flags, I know that toxic relationships like the one I had with Miguel are easy to get addicted to. The oxytocin and dopamine that flood the body, creating deep feelings of attachment, makes it almost too difficult to consider leaving. Knowing this provides some comfort when I reflect on my relationship with Miguel. It is easy to get hooked to the cycle of love-bombing, idealisation, devalue and discard. This cycle really makes your head spin and damages your emotional well-being.

REFLECTION POINTS

Grab a journal or use the notes in the back of the book and write down any of the personality traits that resonate with your partner's behaviour.

Chapter 3

Cracked Eggs!

AFTER YEARS OF WALKING on eggshells and feeling like Miguel's personal servant, I knew I never wanted to repeat that anxiety-provoking and painful relationship with another man. Unfortunately, despite my best efforts, that's exactly what happened, only with a twist.

I moved out of my home with Miguel and met Kyle just 2 weeks later. Kyle was the polar opposite of Miguel, physically, professionally, and in personality. Kyle was a tall man, with a slim build, red hair and green eyes.

He was a plasterer and had applied to the police force where he had aspirations to become a detective. When he showed up to plaster my new home, he told me he was looking for a life change after a recent traumatic divorce. He was charming in a humble introverted way, and at first, Kyle almost seemed insecure, shy, but an all-round nice guy.

I was drawn to Kyle's personality and enjoyed chatting with him. I had no intentions of dating the man plastering my house, but *my first mistake was telling him too much about myself too soon. He studied me through the information I had unwittingly given to him and very quickly he created the persona that would draw me in.* He became my anti-Miguel. Kyle seemed hard-working, liked manual labour and fixing things. He didn't seem to be interested in money, brand names or a flashy lifestyle. Most of all, he seemed kind and gentle. Upon request, he even removed the ladybirds that had created a small colony in my house and set them free outside prior to painting the walls. He was just so sweet! How could this guy be a danger to me? He even showed compassion for ladybirds.

We shared so many interests; a love of travel and cultures, an interest in debating politics and current events, a love of food, we both spoke French, it was uncanny. When I had to leave or was at work, Kyle would take it upon himself to do other things around the house, as a favour, completely free of charge. He would install light fixtures, and update wall sockets. I thought this was great. In five years, Miguel had never changed a light bulb and my plasterer was fitting lights for no extra charge!

One day Kyle shyly asked if I would consider going out for a glass of wine with him. At this time, I was not looking for a relationship, but a distraction. I thought Kyle was a safe pair of hands and just what I needed to avoid thinking about Miguel. That was how our almost four-year-long relationship began.

Even if the new person you meet right after a breakup seems to be a safe bet, you are emotionally all over the place and not ready to be with anyone. In love, safe bets don't really exist either. It is common to look for the exact opposite partner when leaving a toxic relationship. In my case, I still found myself with a narcissist, just a sneaky and deceitful one.

After our relationship had ended, I discovered that Kyle had a history of preying on women who were either recently divorced or leaving bad relationships. His behaviour, in the beginning, made sense: when he met me he saw his next opportunity and looked for ways to weasel his way into my heart.

He told me stories about growing up in a home filled with emotional, physical, verbal, and sexual abuse. He told me stories about how awful and crazy his mother and ex-wife were. According to Kyle, he was raised a Jehovah's Witness and had never celebrated holidays or received birthday presents as a child.

In response to these stories, I wanted to show him that women could be kind, trustworthy, and good. I wanted to give him nice birthdays and Christmas holidays. I wanted us to dress up and celebrate Halloween together. Side note - one year Kyle and I dressed up for Halloween as Little Red Riding Hood and the Big Bad Wolf… wasn't that telling? I really thought he deserved to experience unconditional and pure love and make up for the fun that he said he missed during his childhood.

As a mental health professional, Kyle's combination of life-altering events seems pretty significant to me and I would expect that someone with that past to have some sort of mental health or emotional difficulties, likely severe ones. As a wounded woman looking for love, attention, and validation, I focused on the good and decided to ignore that substantial history of trauma and abuse. This was a huge mistake.

Proceed with caution when starting a relationship with people who have a history of severe mental illness in their family and a history of severe trauma and abuse. It is possible to come from these dysfunctional situations and have healthy lives, but only after years of intensive treatment and counselling. Without years of therapy and treatment, a partner with such a traumatic history could be a very risky choice.

Despite all the neglect and abuse that he had endured, Kyle *seemed* very well-adjusted, nice, and good-natured. My other friends who were psychologists and psychiatrists even commented on how well adjusted he was considering his past. Everyone who met Kyle said he was such a nice, likeable person.

Cracked Eggs

One of my best friends who is a counsellor likes to say that you should treat new partners like eggs at the supermarket. When you open a dozen and you find out that one of the eggs is cracked, you choose another carton. Everyone has baggage and issues, but try not to bring home a cracked egg - a person who is obviously very damaged. It is okay to put the carton with a cracked egg back on the shelf. ***Remember your job is not to piece people back together.*** Your job is to love yourself first before you are able to love others.

My cracked egg, Kyle, treated me like a queen. He couldn't do enough for me. For example, driving at night or in the rain makes me anxious, so Kyle would drive me to see clients, sit in the car for four to six hours, and then drive me home. He did this almost every weekend and sometimes during the week too. Kyle would clean my house and wash the dishes, without me even asking. He would rub my feet at night and shower me with affection and attention.

Idealise, Devalue, Discard

Kyle was also a master at flattery. He constantly told me how pretty, smart and special I was, and what a great cook I was. He also was just so romantic. Surprisingly Miguel never danced with me but Kyle did, and everywhere. Kyle would spin me around and dance with me everywhere; on a street corner, in the middle of a tiny restaurant, at my parents' house. He would make candles for me, bring me flowers, send me love poems. The flattery and romance lasted until the end of our relationship, and I loved it. Who wouldn't like all those compliments and gestures? I only received these compliments and gestures in the very beginning of my relationship with Miguel, and then quickly he picked me apart, insulted me, and devalued me. It felt so good that Kyle seemed to appreciate and love me. It was so nice to feel like I didn't have to walk on eggshells and so wonderful to not get yelled at.

Kyle did have some flaws, which I of course rationalised and brushed off. *He would play a push-pull game with me that I did not understand until our relationship ended.* We would go on a fun vacation and everything appeared to be better than ever. Then Kyle would write me a letter saying how much he loved me but how I was too good for him and how he felt like he was not enough. He said I would be better off without him. He would also say that he felt like there was something wrong with him and that he should be alone. This always seemed to come right out of the blue. I remember thinking what the heck is going on?

Kyle played this push-pull game probably about every six months, and always at very unexpected times, like right after we went to look at engagement rings, right after a very romantic Valentine's Day, right before I had to present my thesis for my master's degree in French. After the relationship ended, I observed a pattern of Kyle building me up to tear me down. Kyle never complained, never got mad, and we never fought but he used passive-aggressive tactics to hurt me.

He would often abandon me right after or before something special. I was completely unaware of this pattern and felt pity for Kyle and would try to convince him that he was good enough and try to help him cure his childhood wounds. I sent him countless articles about childhood trauma and abuse and other self-help information.

I thought, "If I can just fix his trauma then this push-pull stuff will stop." This, of course, was wrong of me. I didn't realise that Kyle was acting like *a very typical narcissist and engaging in a cruel pattern- idealise, devalue and discard.*

One day, Kyle would write me a love letter saying how much he wanted to get married and have a family, and how happy he was living with me. Then, the next day, he wanted out of the relationship and acted cold. The reasons were always the same; he needed to be alone, he wasn't good enough, there was something wrong with him.

He would then disappear for a day, maybe a weekend, and come back and we would work it out and things would get back to normal rather quickly. This created a great deal of cognitive dissonance and reinforced our trauma bond. *Cognitive dissonance is the confusion caused by having two opposite or competing behaviours and values.* When this "pull away" would happen, all I wanted was my super sweet, perfect, kind man back. It was very confusing and fast, like the flip of a switch. He would be here, gone, and then back here again.

During the relationship, I always overlooked how I felt when Kyle would pull away. I idealised his good traits and ignored his bad ones. I never took the time to reflect on how anxious, confused, sad, and upset I would get when Kyle would decide he didn't want to be with me for a few days. I ignored how inconsiderate he was when during his absences he wouldn't answer my calls or texts. I would just always take him back and never think about what was going on.

A specific example was when two of my best psychiatrist friends were driving three hours to meet Kyle and spend the weekend with us. This may have been the first time Kyle discarded me. All week we talked about where we were going to take my friends and what we were going to do over the weekend. Kyle helped me plan the meals I was going to cook and even cleaned the kitchen and living room so the house would be ready for guests. We enjoyed a romantic evening the night before my friends were going to arrive and Kyle told me how much he loved being with me and how happy he was.

The next day, a few hours before my friends arrived, Kyle said that he wasn't coming, that he didn't think he was good enough for me and that he didn't want to meet my friends. I remember thinking what the heck happened? What am I going to tell my friends when they get here? I felt so sad and embarrassed. I remember feeling so confused; why did he help me clean, have sex with me the day before and say how happy he was? What changed in less than 24 hours?

I remember feeling so embarrassed I told my friends that something came up and Kyle couldn't come. Then the next day he showed up to meet my friends with a big smile like everything was normal. He brought me flowers and said he was sorry. Of course, I had guests and didn't want to make the situation seem awkward so I just smiled and pretended like everything was okay.

So I did what I always used to do, I just pretended like it didn't happen. I didn't really follow up after my friends left and tried to forget about Kyle's little disappearing act. I was hoping that it wouldn't happen again. I was hoping that it was a fluke and the dishwashing dancing guy would be back to stay.

Here is a little tip: *when someone tells you or shows you there is something wrong with them, listen. When what they show you becomes a hurtful pattern, run, run, run as fast as you can.* Patterns like this are hard to break and will destroy you emotionally. Also, never send people self-help articles that they don't ask for; in fact, even if they do ask, let them find them by themselves, you'll soon know if they're genuinely motivated or playing games. Read self-help articles for your own benefit. *Always focus on your own growth and healing, not other peoples'. We can only heal ourselves.*

Compartmentalisation

I rationalised other things that were red flags with my second narcissist. Kyle was one of 4 children and all his siblings lived in the same town as us. His parents lived there too. *In almost four years, I only met a handful of his family, even though they all lived within a twenty-minute drive of my house.*

Kyle knew all of my family, including extended family, and all of my friends, including those who lived out of town or out of the country. He would spend holidays with us. Kyle would call my family and friends on their birthdays. We would go out to eat and have dinner parties. I would invite his family over to visit and Kyle would say they were too crazy or wouldn't accept me due to their beliefs. In my denial, I thought that Kyle avoided people who hurt him and made him think of his traumatic childhood. Selfishly, it was nice I did not have to share him during holidays, or with his family. So, I did what I used to do when something seemed off - I let it go and didn't think about it too much. I looked on the bright side, which was having him all to myself, which never really was the case! Kyle should really write a book about multitasking; he was quite good at it!

If someone seems to compartmentalise where you fit into their life, question that right away. If your partner seems to hide you or isolate you from your loved ones or their loved ones, don't accept that. This isn't the behaviour of someone in a loving relationship and is almost always a sign of dysfunction or abuse. If you feel like you are being hidden in a serious relationship, there is something wrong. There is never a reason to hide your partner in a healthy relationship.

These were just some of the covert signs that Kyle was a master manipulator and a true narcissist. Eventually, I found out that Kyle was living a double and sometimes triple life. This is still confusing to me because it seemed like we were always together and like I always knew where he was. Kyle confessed to having unprotected sex with 10 girls during our relationship. He would rotate women who his family and friends got to meet. I still find this mind-boggling how he pulled this off.

Kyle had a green truck that he bought about a year into our relationship that I knew nothing about, so he could cheat in our small market town without getting caught easily. He shared his location on his phone with me so I thought I always knew where he was, but he would leave his phone one place and go somewhere else. He lied about working extra shifts once he was in the force when he was actually having multiple affairs on the side.

One day I found a box of women's clothes and pictures in the garage. Kyle confessed to having serious issues with addictions, being in serious relationships with multiple women at the same time, and being a pathological liar. Kyle also confessed to making up terrible lies about me engaging in criminal activity, being violent and abusive, to keep his other girlfriends away from me. He confessed all of these things with no remorse or emotion. I am guessing he confessed because I confronted him with proof and it was almost impossible to lie at that point. It was like a stranger I never met was telling me these horrible stories. Kyle's exact words to me were, "I did these things to you because I am a psychopath."

It was like getting punched in the stomach and a feeling of total numbness to accept that Kyle, who for years I considered to be the best guy I ever met, was actually far worse than mean Miguel.

Connecting The Dots

So how did I feel when I finally connected all the dots? After the confession, I felt stunned. For a few weeks, I played detective and wanted to figure out the truth and know what to expect. I talked to his ex-wife, who had a very similar experience and sold her business because Kyle ruined her reputation with rumours and lies. I wanted to talk to the girls in the pictures, I wanted to know what the heck was going on. What I didn't want was to talk to Kyle.

My feelings would fluctuate a lot; somedays I felt scared, some days I felt sad, somedays I felt angry. I almost always felt anxious. I would constantly ask myself questions like, "How stable is this guy?" "What else could he do to me?" "Was all of this just an act and a game?" "How could he do this after everything he knew about Miguel?" After a few months, I had some clarity and could see all of the little things that made me realise Kyle really wasn't such a great guy at all. I was able to take apart all those push-pull episodes, the patterns, and the times when Kyle's excuses didn't make sense.

Kyle was different from Miguel, in so many ways that I missed the red flags and signs from my previous relationship. *I was in denial about Kyle abusing me, manipulating me and hurting me.* The truth of the relationship wasn't clear until after the relationship was over. With Miguel, I knew it all along. I just wasn't ready to admit it or leave. I rationalised and excused both their behaviours and hoped things would change. There were subtle things that Kyle would say or do that were hurtful or confusing during our relationship. Looking back, there were times when things did not feel right, but I ignored my intuition. Here is another tip: do not ignore your intuition about people, it is usually right.

Kyle's Red Flags

Kyle's covert narcissistic personality traits that I ignored or did not discover until the relationship ended:

- Sharing intimate details of his personal life very quickly
- Acting like a knight in shining armour, going to extremes to rescue and fix things

- Being overly nice and agreeable
- Liking everything that I liked
- Subtle efforts to look for praise, recognition, and acceptance
- Excessive need for affection and physical touch
- Subtly looking for pity
- Anxious behaviour out in public, always looking over his shoulder, wanting to face the door in public places
- Subtly putting me down or finding flaws in me about things I could not change
- Intense eye gazes and at times blank eye gazes as if he was disconnected
- Distractibility
- Promising and planning a wonderful future life that he had no intentions of providing
- Excessive shallow flattery instead of genuine compliments
- Deceitful
- Mirroring my behaviours and speech
- Seeming to be overly sensitive, understanding or empathetic to my needs
- Lack of respect for social rules
- Risk-taking behaviour such as drinking and driving and unprotected sex with multiple partners
- Impulsive purchases
- Dishonesty about money
- Alcohol abuse
- Not introducing me to family and friends
- Calculated behaviours and lies to keep up multiple lives
- Compartmentalising people in his life
- Subtle shifts in personality when around different people
- Push-pull cycles

- Idealisation, devalue and discard
- Lying about small and big things
- Tuning out, excessive daydreaming
- Making up stories to make current and former loved ones look bad
- Playing the victim
- Excessive interest in weapons, firearms, and professions where you have power and control
- Cruelty to animals (Kyle killed his mother's beloved cat as a child: I know, how did I let that one go?)
- Risk-taking and rule-breaking behaviour
- Stealing

Chapter 4

Self Praise is no Recommendation

WE HAVE ALREADY ESTABLISHED that most Cluster B personalities have fragile egos that require constant tending to. Attention-seeking behaviour is often displayed by these personalities in ways that feed their need to be seen, heard and in many cases respected, whether earned or not. They also engage in these behaviours as a way of compensating for their lack of a true sense of self. Interestingly, both negative and positive attention serves as a supply for this personality type.

The grandiose behaviour that we often associate with narcissists is usually quite obvious and easily identified. The overt narcissist tends to seek attention with designer labels, well-known brand names, fancy cars, titles, money, and other external means of recognition. The grandiose narcissist, when in a relationship, is often the boastful partner who seems to do more talking than listening in any conversation. They have a tendency to exaggerate and stretch the truth in their pursuit of attention and validation.

If you have read up to this point, then you can probably guess that Miguel presented grandiosity and many overt attention-seeking behaviours. Even though Miguel seemed to be very confident in his image and his career, he required a great deal of praise and recognition. He would become quite angry if I didn't notice or compliment him constantly for his achievements. If Miguel won an award or was recognised at work he would always ask me, "Did you tell your parents, what did they say?" "Did you tell your friends, what did they say?" Miguel was brilliant, he was intelligent and professionally accomplished, and he often deserved the praise that he sought from others; however, the extent to which he needed to be praised and recognised was rather problematic and honestly a big turn-off for me.

Miguel knew that his status as a doctor would draw the attention of women. Miguel would flirt and talk with females all the time, in front of me and undoubtedly behind my back, feeding his ego and desire for attention. Miguel would come home after a long day at work and brag about the nurses and hospital workers who were in love with him. This obviously made me feel jealous and insecure, but I let it go to avoid confrontation.

It became quite apparent that Miguel's need for validation was so great that he couldn't actually operate in a social setting without it. I quickly learned that telling him how handsome he was, how well-dressed he was and how smart he was, were daily requirements. Even though I flattered his ego the best that I could, Miguel would frequently say things like, "I know you think I am ugly," or, "I know you don't think being a doctor is a big deal, but a lot of other women do." I'm not sure if Miguel was just fishing for compliments or if his ego was so fragile that my love and compliments didn't touch the level of attention his fragile ego needed to thrive.

Let's move on to Kyle and his covert attention-seeking strategies. To be fair to Kyle, he was also brilliant in his own way. Kyle was very good at deceiving and manipulating people, so much so that I eventually became convinced that he liked, said, and did the exact opposite of what was really going on. If you are a survivor of a relationship with a covert narcissist, then you probably understand what I am getting at here. He had me convinced during our relationship that attention made him feel uncomfortable and that he was a very modest guy. Kyle convinced everyone that he was a humble, kind, and empathetic guy. In previous chapters, I explained how Kyle would do selfless acts of service and seemed to want to really put himself out to help others. Now, looking back on things, I realise that this was clearly not the reality; the truth was, Kyle loved praise, even though he denied it, and he went to extreme efforts to get attention.

After Kyle's lies unravelled, he admitted that he had a very fragile ego. In my opinion, *Kyle's generosity toward others, acts of service, and the illusion he created of the good honest Scotsman were just ploys to get attention and stroke his fragile ego.* Actually, I think he considered extreme acts of service as the only way he could get recognition. As I described in previous chapters, Kyle was insecure about his lack of formal education; he was homeschooled as a child and cut off from much of the world by extremely religious parents. According to Kyle, his mother struggled to raise four boys and had mental health issues of her own to deal with; as a result, the children received very little academic instruction and spent most of their time working on the farm or at church.

Kyle never had the income potential, fancy degrees, titles, or social mobility that Miguel had. During our relationship, Kyle told me that this made him feel very insecure and that he was not good enough. I believe the only way Kyle knew or thought he could get praise or attention was by doing and giving to others. Even though he said he didn't like praise or recognition, Kyle would leave thank you cards he would get from charities for some "good deed" laying around so I would make a fuss over what a great guy he was. He would use statements like, "Wow, I wish I was as smart as you," to fish for compliments. I felt guilty and sad that Kyle didn't feel good enough and went out of my way to compliment him and make him feel special.

In addition to playing up his victim role in his family and first marriage, Kyle looked for attention in other ways. Kyle had an insatiable desire for physical touch. I have never met or observed another human being who needed to be touched, rubbed, held, kissed and hugged as much as Kyle. His other lovers have confirmed he was the same way with them, too. When I was with Kyle, he would become sad if he was not getting constant physical affection, and when people were around, he would really turn up his romantic side. He would put music on and dance with me in the kitchen in front of guests, excessively flattering and complimenting me. When Kyle behaved in this way most people would smile and say things like, "What a romantic guy, isn't she lucky?" "I wish my boyfriend treated me like that." On other occasions, Kyle's displays were so over the top, that they would make my guests and I very uncomfortable. Nevertheless, this was how Kyle got attention and his fragile narcissistic ego got fed. I thought it was about his love for me but these acts were about Kyle's love for himself.

Another interesting point worth mentioning is that you are also a form of attention and narcissistic supply for this type of partner. *If you are in a relationship with a narcissist the odds are that you are something special. They wouldn't pick you if you weren't.* Remember, image is everything to Cluster B personality types, and they are going to choose a partner who will enhance their image. Their preferred type tends to be smart, competent, loving, kind, wealthy and beautiful. Please remember this if your self-esteem has taken a hit from your relationship.

Having said that, I am the first to declare that I am no supermodel and I am definitely flawed; however, I do believe that both Miguel and Kyle considered me to be their trophies. Miguel liked to show me off to his family and friends - my European features, education and ability to speak more than one language made me excellent wife material to his family and friends.

When it came to Kyle, as I mentioned previously, his Achilles heel was his lack of formal education and social mobility, as a result of his upbringing. On occasion Kyle liked to show me off to his workmates; even commenting on how much money I made and how simple his friends' wives and girlfriends were.

Even though at times it made him feel uncomfortable and confused, Kyle would brag at work about how much I got paid, how many languages I spoke, and where I went to school. Kyle bragged and showed me off because it was a way for him to get more attention. Kyle wasn't proud of me, he was proud of himself for being with me.

So why did I tolerate these attention-seeking behaviours from my partners? The answer as always is firmly rooted in my childhood. As a child, I was always taught to put the needs of others first. I was taught that this made me a good person, and no one wants to be a bad person, right? I was taught to compliment others and not focus on myself or my achievements. I can still hear my grandmother telling me that, "Self-praise is no recommendation." Looking for attention or compliments in any way was strongly discouraged in my family while it was encouraged to compliment others.

I didn't learn to be selfish or focus on my needs; instead, I became a people-pleaser. *In my house, giving and doing for others was the gold standard and putting everyone else ahead of you was always the admirable choice.* Kyle and Miguel wanted and needed attention, so I gave it to them even when it made me feel uncomfortable. I catered to all of their needs first even when I didn't want to. That is what I thought a good partner in a relationship did, now I know this is wrong.

Red Flags for Cluster B personality attention-seeking behaviours:

- High interest in their image
- High interest in material things
- Spending money they don't have to maintain their image
- Constant fishing for compliments
- Always bragging and boasting
- Showing off in front of others
- Exaggerating stories to get attention
- Extreme acts of kindness to get attention
- Showing off friends and girlfriends who have accomplishments to get attention
- Hiding people in their lives who do not reflect well on them
- Tantrum-like behaviour when they do not get attention

REFLECTION POINTS

- What does a healthy need for attention look like to you?
- Did you get enough attention and praise as a child?

PART 2

"I don't care what you think unless it is about me."

—KURT COBAIN

Chapter 5

Meet Prince Charming

A TYPICAL TRAIT OF overt narcissistic partners is the ability to pull their love interest in with charisma and charm. These toxic people are experts at acting and creating a likeable image. They can often present as the life of the party and an expert with words, always knowing the right thing to say.

On the other hand, more covert charmers may present as very unique, kind, exciting and mysterious individuals. It's also not unusual for a Cluster B personality to show up as a lovely, attentive, humble caretaker in the first instance, in an attempt to win you over.

My first narcissist, Miguel, had a kilowatt smile that anyone would notice across a room. He was a sharp dresser and a loud talker. He loved being the centre of attention. Miguel was also the guy who would buy rounds of drinks for everyone at the bar. My friends would comment that when we first started dating, you could see the sparks and connection in his gaze when he would look at me. Miguel just had a presence and confidence about him that was undeniable. He appeared to be intimidated by no one and always knew what to say and do in every social situation. He was so smooth.

Miguel also used his charming ways to get what he wanted with ease. Somehow, during his medical residency, Miguel ended up living with my grandparents and paying virtually nothing for his keep. He also convinced my family and friends, many of whom work in healthcare, that this was normal and a good thing because he could keep an eye on the elderly couple.

My mother cooked for Miguel daily and bought him clothes for years. He would call my parents "mummy" and "daddy" just like I did. He would hug my mother and also flatter her always. I ended up being sweet-talked into lending Miguel over £20,000 during the first years of our relationship; financing his vacations, wardrobe, and cars. Miguel was a master manipulator, a true expert at convincing people to do things for him.

If you have had no experience with a person who is a narcissist, you may be thinking, "How did this guy fool you and your family?" You may also be wondering, "Why would you want to be in a relationship with such a parasite?" However, I am guessing that if you are reading this book, you probably have some experience or a curiosity about how this personality type can manipulate, use and take advantage of others. An expert charmer like Miguel and a people-pleaser with poor boundaries like myself made a very dysfunctional couple.

The Disney effect

Society teaches us that we should want a prince or a princess who is charming, confident and who will sweep us off of our feet. Films and TV programmes, children's books and adult novels bombard us with this image from an early age; framing our beliefs about romance and romantic partners, promoting the idea of unrealistic happily-ever-afters.

In my case, an intelligent bi-lingual handsome doctor, who was loving, affectionate, and attentive in the beginning, was hard to give up. This type of partner is precisely the kind of person that my family wanted for me; they had set us up after all. I always struggled to maintain healthy boundaries with my family and to say 'no' to them. Due to me being a people-pleaser, often avoiding confrontations and challenging discussions, when I did start to feel like something wasn't right, I stayed in the relationships to avoid disappointing them.

Miguel appeared to be a Disney Prince. He was likeable and charming; people valued his intelligence, appearance and successful career. Unfortunately, *he slowly began to turn from a prince into a toad; his short temper, tantrums and selfishness were becoming difficult to ignore.*

The Martyr

Kyle, on the other hand, kept his narcissism mostly hidden until the very end. Now and then, I would get a glimpse of his toxicity, but he always managed to charm and flatter his way out of any potential conflict. It is interesting to think that Kyle, who had no formal education, was much more sophisticated and intelligent in his abuse tactics than Miguel with his fancy degrees and titles.

Kyle's charm was subtle and low key. He was captivating but in a less showy and more humble way. He never wanted to be the centre of attention, but instead wanted to make whomever he met feel like the centre of attention. While Miguel was quick to boast about his accolades, Kyle would fawn over the achievements of others, especially mine.

Kyle was the kind of guy who would go out of his way to speak to people, meeting them on their level, demonstrating his fake empathy and humility. *Kyle was the guy who appeared to self-sacrifice, putting others first and appearing to be a bit of a martyr.* He was an expert at presenting himself as a non-threatening, caring, Scottish gentleman. I later came to discover that he was an expert liar, skilled at dividing his time and compartmentalising the people in his life, for his benefit.

Kyle was skilled with flattery and seemed to give out so many compliments. This was a constant in our relationship. *He never insulted me, yelled at me, or talked down to me directly. Coming off of my relationship with Miguel, in which his flattery quickly turned into insults and verbal abuse, I ate up every lovely word I could get from Kyle.* It made me feel validated and special. Too bad I didn't know all the awful things he said behind my back sooner. Everyone liked Kyle. Even though he made way less money, was far less educated, and had the more problematic past and family, everyone wanted me to be with him and liked him more than they did Miguel.

Kyle would sometimes look at me and just say, "Wow, you are so pretty," look down and smile like a bashful teenager. He would pretend the little things about me were so captivating to him and unique when they weren't anything special. Kyle seemed to love everything about me; and, it would appear, my friends, family and even my dog. Kyle went as far as to tell me how in love he was with my dog and how she had the prettiest face. He would always make such a fuss of her, making sure I knew how much he adored her. I later found out that Kyle had told one of his other lady friends how much he hated my puppy.

Kyle would also flatter and compliment my best friends, saying how nice they were and what good friends they were to me. Later on in the relationship whenever he would have an episode, he would declare how uncomfortable my social circle made him feel; he was so contrary, I often didn't know where I stood with him.

We have established that narcissists use superficial charm to obtain what they want. I'm not referring to people who are naturally and genuinely charming; those who have a way about them and make people feel unique from a genuine place. I am referring to the act of uncovering someone's weakness and exploiting it through words, actions and whatever else to get their way.

It's important to understand that these toxic individuals do everything to meet their own needs, to stroke their egos, to make themselves feel good. What I fell in love with was an illusion, not a real person. I never really knew either one of these abusive men. Sadly, I'm not really sure that they even fully knew who they were. Their lives of constant lies and manipulations prevent them from truly loving themselves or feeling healthy love for anyone else.

One of the questions that I had to ask myself during recovery was why did I respond the way I did to positive attention? Why did I melt and get so hooked over compliments and some flowers and chocolate? Why was hearing nice things more powerful than having someone hurt me? Looking back at childhood, my parents didn't really give me many compliments. Honestly, maybe it was a cultural part of when and where I grew up because my friends didn't get them either. If I would come home with a 97% on a test the first thing my parents would say was, "Good, next time get a 98%." If I would ever boast about talent or achievement I would hear, "There is always someone better than you out there, be humble." As a child, my parents expected me to deliver top grades at school, help out around the home and be a good girl. There were consequences for not doing these things but little recognition when I achieved them.

I often wonder if this is why as an adult I fell so hard for praise and compliments and looked to be recognised by my partners.

Chapter 6

It's not a Competition

IF YOU HAVE HAD the misfortune of being in a relationship with a narcissistic partner, then you may be familiar with the constant put-downs made in an attempt to make you feel inferior to them.

If you have ever wondered why they were with you even though you weren't 'good enough' for them, stop. The problem isn't you, it is them, and their constant need to feel better about themselves.

Narcissists typically suffer from low self-worth, a lack of self-awareness and, despite their outward shows of confidence, they are usually lacking confidence deep down inside.

One of the ways a Cluster B personality tries to cope with his fragile ego is to project any insecurities onto their partner. They are known to be easily offended, hold grudges, and be hypercritical of others. They work tirelessly to portray themselves as superior and more important than everyone else they meet, while deep inside, they feel the exact opposite.

Miguel made it clear in private and in public that he thought he was smarter than me. Even when it came to issues related to psychology, Miguel made it clear that he went to medical school and therefore he knew more than me about everything related to mental health. If I had a different opinion about a subject matter, Miguel was quick to attack my thinking because I was intellectually inferior. Miguel also liked to remind me that he was the attractive one in the relationship and criticised everything about my image; hair, makeup, clothing, body, everything!

Miguel also believed that he deserved special treatment - often showing how offended he was if I did not buy him the most expensive gifts. He would expect me to cook restaurant-quality meals three times a day while working full time. Miguel viewed me and anyone else in his life as inferior, and he would throw a tantrum and become verbally aggressive when anyone rejected or disobeyed his requests.

If Miguel could not sleep at night, he would wake me up because he thought it was unfair if I was resting and he wasn't. It could be two in the morning on a work night and he would shake my shoulders until I would wake up and keep him company in his insomnia. If Miguel was hot, he would turn the temperature of the house down to freezing levels, even if we had guests over who complained about the cold, what mattered most was that Miguel was comfortable. Miguel insisted on buying me gifts that he liked or approved of, not what I wanted or needed. These gifts were usually clothes or jewellery that were of his liking.

When Miguel would travel to "visit family" he frequently would get home at one or two in the morning. He would demand that I stay up and be waiting to have sex with him wearing new lingerie, knowing that I had to wake up at five in the morning for work. I did try to talk to him about this once in a nice way, saying that we could wait until the next day, that I was tired; instead, he scolded me for being selfish. So to avoid making him angry, I'd go out, buy something new and stay up. Little did I know he was returning from a trip where he was visiting a girlfriend and probably seeing lots of new lingerie. Miguel thought his way was the best way and the only way in all situations. Miguel lived by his own set of social norms and rules that only applied to him.

During our relationship, I would have said that Kyle struggled to put himself and his needs first. I considered him to be too giving and even suggested that he thought about his own needs, wants, and desires more. Kyle would frequently put on a pity act, saying he was not deserving or good enough for me. Now I know that the other women heard the exact same line. I believe he said these things so we would point out just how special and wonderful we thought he was. As I said in an earlier chapter, Kyle was much more sophisticated in how he manipulated, controlled, and abused, to the point that I wasn't aware that the majority of the manipulation or abuse was even occurring.

Kyle used his religious upbringing, and his relationship with God to show himself to be morally and spiritually superior to me. Kyle would share stories about giving to a charity or helping a homeless person on the street, making sure his good deeds received plenty of praise from myself and others while bolstering his fragile ego. Kyle would routinely suggest that I do more for others, pointing out my lack of charitable deeds.

Kyle also expressed entitlement in other ways. I would notice when we would house sit for friends that Kyle would take clothes to wear and eat food from my friends' homes freely. When I told him that it was not okay to wear my friend's pants while we were housesitting, he didn't seem to understand what was socially strange about going into someone's bedroom, opening a drawer, and putting on a pair of their pants. Kyle would also tell me stories about taking sweets and food from people's houses while on a plastering job. I always thought these were bold moves, bordering on stealing. Kyle didn't seem to see anything wrong with his behaviours; he justified it by saying he only ever took small things, like a packet of biscuits, a phone charger, loose change here and there.

Kyle's need for superiority was also shown in how he struggled with being around accomplished people. Kyle also complained about me making more money, being better educated and being a working professional.

Kyle said he felt like I didn't need him the way most women in the past did and how this was upsetting to him. Of course, I told him how he was so nice and so smart and how everyone including me saw that. I think what Kyle was getting at was that he was afraid that he could not control me the way he controlled other women. Of course in the moment these comments all went right over my head.

Kyle frequently said that it was very important to him to feel superior, more intelligent, and more dominant than his sexual partners. Kyle expressed how he always needed his sexual partners to trust him and need him to turn him on. I did always find these statements weird but I let it go.

After the relationship ended I heard how Kyle would belittle me behind my back. He would frequently make fun of me and put me down. To my face, Kyle would say how my salary, education and job were intimidating to him but behind my back, he would mock how he took advantage of me financially and didn't have any respect for my career or intelligence. Kyle to my face would also frequently say that he felt like the "ugly one" in the relationship but behind my back, he made it very clear that he perceived me to be the less attractive one.

Reflecting on the issues with entitlement, superiority and self-importance that my two narcissists had, my biggest takeaway is that your partner should make you feel good about yourself. *One of my dear therapist friends always tells her clients to surround themselves with people who build them up, not tear them down. A relationship should not be a competition.* Your partner should not feel insecure about your accomplishments or skills. You should value your partner's strengths and support them in areas in which you are stronger. If you feel like your partner is always asking and taking and not giving enough, they probably are. If they seem to only be giving in order to make themselves look good, they probably are. A relationship is about, give and take, and supporting one another. It should never be all about you or all about them.

As I reflect on this chapter, *the importance of establishing healthy boundaries in a relationship also stands out.* If something makes you feel uncomfortable, it is a good idea to tell your partner about it. If you feel like you are being treated unfairly, you need to express your concern. If you do not want to do something, it's okay to not do it. Issues with boundaries, people-pleasing and bending over backwards to try to make my loved ones happy were something that was modelled for me and also expected of me, during childhood. These behaviours take processing and time to be unlearned. If you struggle with setting boundaries and people-pleasing like me, you can and will learn new, healthier ways.

Red flags of entitlement, superiority and self-importance:

- Put-downs
- Insulting intelligence
- Criticising physical appearance
- Grandiose sense of importance
- Unrealistic and inconsiderate expectations
- Need for special treatment
- Thinking rules and social norms don't apply to them

- Putting their needs first - always
- Need to feel superior
- Struggle with being wrong, contradicted, or different views

Chapter 7

Love Languages?

YOU MAY OR MAY not be familiar with the term 'love-bombing'. Think excessive compliments, gifts, and expressions of affection; to the point where you start to ask WHY??!!?? You may be wondering what the problem is. Unfortunately, love-bombing is a powerful way of developing trauma bonds with a new or existing partner. Similar to superficial charm, love-bombing is a common trait that many narcissists share.

Everyone experiences love-bombing differently. Like with all relationships with toxic individuals, there is no exact protocol for how your abuser may do this. Each abuser's intentions during the love-bombing stage may be different as well. They are not all that important. Some may feel infatuated and obsessed with you and feel the need to be around you all the time to try to attach to you. Some may think that they are in love, and this time their relationship will be genuine and different. Some may 'love-bomb' to suck you in and to set the stage for future manipulation and control.

As I stated earlier, don't spend too much time focusing on a mentally ill person's intentions or analysing them: it will not change or solve anything. Accept that insanity does not have a logical explanation, and leave it there. Focus on the result, which is that the love-bombing attached you to your ex-partner, confused you and ultimately hurt you. Focus on your feelings during and after the love-bombing. Forgive yourself for connecting to someone who did not have pure intentions.

Getting hooked during love-bombing is very easy to do. It is natural to hope that this new person is lovely and it's expected to like being showered with attention and affection. Here is your next tip: extreme acts of kindness, generosity, love, and attention, especially early in a relationship, are red flags. Learn from this and be aware of it in the future. Forgive yourself for believing them and wanting their actions to be genuine. Focus on your feelings during and after love-bombing to help you heal.

I experienced the love-bombing phase differently with each narcissist. Miguel started his love-bombing with gifts, flowers and lots of attention. The attention quickly turned dark. During the first few months of our relationship, Miguel and I would talk on the phone for hours; well, he would talk, and I would listen for hours. It was not unusual for Miguel to demand three to four hours of phone conversations daily when we first met. Sometimes, I would take my dog for a twenty-minute walk and leave my phone at home; I would come home to find thirty missed calls. Miguel acted so concernedly, worried and upset if I did not answer the phone or respond to a text immediately. Eventually, he became verbally abusive or gave me the silent treatment if I did not respond right away.

Miguel also expected me to spend a lot of time with him very early in our relationship. When we first started dating, I lived and worked 1.5 hours away from him. He wanted to see me every weekend and at least one or two days during the week. Considering that he was completing his medical residency and I was working full time, this was an unrealistic expectation. Miguel was new to the country, but he never developed any real friendships at the hospital where he worked. When he was not with me, he would want to visit and spend time with my family, even if I wasn't there.

Miguel would also become angry if I wanted to hang out with friends instead of spending time with him. I did not like how I would feel when Miguel was angry or disappointed in me. I gave in to his demands to avoid conflict. I tended to freeze and dissociate from what was going on when Miguel got angry. I learned this coping skill during childhood and practised it when faced with uncomfortable situations throughout my adult life.

A few months after Miguel and I started dating, I remember visiting him one weekend and telling him about a summer trip to Italy that I was planning with one of my girlfriends. The relationship was very new, and I thought his response would be positive. I remember sitting on his bed rummaging through my purse for my phone casually describing some hotels I was looking into in Rome when the screaming started. Miguel told me that if I was going to leave the country, it was going to be with him. That I was an adult and it was immature for me to go on girls' trips. Then I got the typical Miguel comment "What about me? What am I going to do when you are in Italy?"

I was not expecting this reaction at all. Miguel told me that I was not going to Italy and then didn't speak to me for the rest of the night. I felt anxious, defeated and a little confused, so I sat quietly and said nothing. Of course, I rationalised his behaviour, thinking he was stressed at work and decided that I would do my best to enjoy what was left of the weekend.

Deep down, I knew Miguel's behaviour was extreme and abnormal in the early stages of a relationship. I was not comfortable spending all my time with Miguel, but I did it anyway. I did not like his temper tantrums. Early on, *I wish I would have paused and made a list of the pros and cons of the relationship or shared the details of Miguel's tantrums with more friends and family.* I wish I would have stopped to ask myself what I was feeling and why I was staying with Miguel. But I didn't. I just avoided thinking about these things and hoped he would change.

Miguel's behaviour was reinforced over time, as he became increasingly explosive and volatile with me. Whenever he realised he had gone too far, the love-bombing phase would start again; there would be gifts, attention, and affection. The cycle would always end with very controlling and demanding behaviours; this went on for over four years.

I wish I had listened to my intuition and walked away early on in the relationship once I had noticed that my needs weren't being met. I wish I hadn't always given in to make him happy or to avoid conflict. I wish I had known then that just because someone is kind to you or buys you gifts, you don't owe them anything in return.

My love-bombing phase with Kyle was utterly different. As with all things, Kyle, his love-bombing was subtle, sweet, and humble. He never seemed controlling. He didn't get angry if I couldn't devote all of my time and attention to him. Kyle would encourage me to spend time with friends and family and act genuinely happy when I had fun plans. I now know he was probably happy because he was free to go and visit his other girlfriends.

The unique thing about Kyle at the beginning of our relationship was that he mirrored my behaviour and expressed a desire to take things slow and not jump into anything serious. I actually referred to him as my friend Kyle for about six months. From early on he knew about my struggles with Miguel and became the anti-Miguel in every way. At times I even felt like I pursued Kyle more than he pursued me.

Kyle love-bombed me by paying attention to details and giving me small, thoughtful gifts; little treats that he knew were important to me, such as candles, my favourite tea, flowers, my favourite chocolates and ice-cream. Kyle would write me love notes and leave cards on the front seat of my car. Kyle also knew that helping me around the house, fixing things, doing favours for me, and taking the initiative without asking were things I longed for in my relationship. I believe Kyle's love-bombing started slowly and got stronger in due time. This could be because I was not his primary source of narcissistic supply at the beginning of the relationship; when I became his main girlfriend, he turned things up a notch.

Kyle also showered me with acts of service, attention and affection. He drove almost two hours after it had snowed to shovel my parents' driveway. Kyle would drive me to appointments during his free time and waited in the car while I visited patients. He seemed happy to help and would request to be my chauffeur. Kyle helped my friends and my friends' family members move multiple times. He would do handyman jobs for my friends for free or for a small fee. He would take it upon himself to buy and fix things around my house before he lived there. Kyle knew that acts of service were one of the ways to my heart.

I felt that Kyle put me on a pedestal and always praised me to my family, friends, and whoever would listen. After the relationship was over, it was very painful to realise that Kyle told terrible lies about me to others during our relationship. Reflecting on the constant praise and flattery and then learning about the cruel rumours that Kyle spread about me created an enormous amount of cognitive dissonance.

Kyle also knew that physical touch and quality time were other ways to make me feel loved, and he showered me with both. Friends would comment about feeling uncomfortable around Kyle and me because he liked to indulge in PDA [public displays of affection]. We went to couples counselling for a while, and even our therapist commented on how Kyle would be all over me during sessions. When we were alone together, which was often, Kyle was very affectionate and would always flatter me. Kyle was often attached to me at the hip when we were together.

Strangely, even though Kyle seemed obsessed with hugging, kissing, cuddling, and dancing in the kitchen with me, I thought he had a relatively low sex drive. We did not have sex a lot during our relationship- maybe once a week- and we waited months before being intimate and would often go through dry spells. Kyle seemed to prefer to cuddle, touch, and kiss. Maybe the other girls tired him out! He would tell me that even though he found me to be so pretty and loved my body that it was hard for him to have sex with me. Kyle told me he preferred to have sex with girls to whom he felt physically and intellectually superior. This may make more sense when we get to the chapter about infidelity and promiscuity.

Kyle was never aggressive, violent or controlling with me. For years, he treated me like a queen and I thought he was the best guy I had ever met. I loved the way he took care of me and how he spoiled me. I was blinded by his excessive kindness, attention and affection.

Looking back on my childhood I always dreamt of someone who would take care of me like my dad took care of my mum. When I met Kyle, I felt like I found someone very similar to my father, with the bonus of a loving romantic touch. I really believed that Kyle was all I ever wanted in a man. Since Kyle combined acts of service, caretaking, and romance, his love-bombing turned into a drug that I didn't want to give up.

Red flags from my love-bombing phases with my two narcissists:

- Excessive communication
- Request to spend all our time together
- Over the top flattery
- Superficial compliments were given out of context
- Lots of gifts, love notes, and romantic outings early on
- Sharing private and confidential information early on
- Taking on the role of my protector, caretaker or saviour

REFLECTION POINTS

- What aspects of love-bombing resonate with you?
- What would you consider acceptable demonstrations of love or affection early on in a relationship?
- How will you manage love-bombing in the future?

Chapter 8

It Was All A Dream...

HAVE YOU EVER MET someone who shares all of your dreams and visions for life? Someone who makes it seem like their only purpose in life is to make sure you have your dream life? Unfortunately, this is probably a sign that they are future-faking. This is a lesser-known term that shows up relentlessly in relationships with narcissists. Future-faking is the making of plans and promises with no intention of keeping either. A classic example would be talking about engagement, marriage and life as a married couple, in great detail. A narcissistic partner will paint this almost as a fairytale, detailing the ins and outs as if they had thought it through and were emotionally committed to the idea. This personality type will often study their partner to find out what their hopes and dreams are, so they know exactly how to 'future-fake' them. Once they have learned about their partners' life goals, values, and what is important to them, they will either act as though they share the same goals and values or promise to provide them. Typically, when the time comes for them to carry out their promises, they make excuses, postpone them, or completely go back on their word.

The very nature of future-faking makes it a great way to manipulate and control partners and their friends and family. *Often narcissists will involve those closest to their partner, embellishing the details and getting their buy-in, to ensure the veracity of the future-faking plan,* making sure the partner is hopeful and has belief in the relationship. Hope is a very powerful emotion and is one of the reasons that partners will stay committed in a relationship that is otherwise toxic. Future-faking also creates cognitive dissonance for the survivor; creating confusion, unfounded excitement and happiness, that one day disappears in an instant. This is heartbreaking. If you have been in a relationship with a narcissist, I am sure you can relate to future-faking and how this made you feel. I'm willing to bet that many of your ex's promises gave you the motivation to stay in the relationship and overlook the red flags.

One of the things that we need to do when a relationship ends is to grieve. When a relationship ends with a "future-faker" we need to grieve the hopes and dreams that we had too. A lot of times these partners sell illusions of who they are, what their intentions are, and the future they will provide or build with their partner. It is painful to accept that what they sold us was all fake. Just because those promises did not materialise, it doesn't mean that the loss cannot be grieved. If you are struggling with processing future-faking take some time to grieve but hold on to your dreams because they can still happen, with a partner who isn't toxic.

In both of my relationships, I lived through future-faking. They both used this strategy to manipulate me and keep me around. I now know they had no intention of following through with any of the promises they made. Miguel and Kyle used future-faking techniques with my family, my friends, and me. Of course, this made me think that they must have been really serious about the relationship and their promises because they told other people about them. This was an area where both Miguel and Kyle were the same.

They both spoke in-depth about getting married, I never brought the subject up. *Miguel and Kyle both took me to look at engagement rings. They both told me they had already planned all the details of the proposal and how impressed I was going to be. Miguel and Kyle both talked about wedding details, babies and future plans way more than I ever did.* Both of them brought up the topic of children and even picked the names for our future children. Both of them talked about the kind of home we would eventually build in great detail. They would tell my family and friends about these plans too and talk about how excited they were about their futures with me. Both even had plans for retirement with me and what we would do with all that free time and how we would save our money. The details and attention they put into these subject matters had me convinced that both Miguel and Kyle were very invested in me and our relationship. What guy would plan out all this stuff so meticulously if they weren't? Now I know the answer, a narcissist.

I never got engaged or married to either of them. There were no romantic proposals. I did live with both of them, but we never bought or built the home of our dreams together. We never had children. I was always told it was coming soon, I just needed to wait for X, Y or Z to happen. Nothing ever happened. What was hurtful was that they used future-faking excuses to cheat such as working extra shifts to save for rings, houses and weddings when they weren't working at all. Kyle wrote me a love letter telling me how excited he was to marry me and start his life with me one day and literally the next he got up and left without any warning to be with two other women - yes, not one, but two.

If you are a woman in your 30s like me and had two "future-faking" men in your life one after the other, you probably feel defeated. Me too. I felt like Miguel and Kyle sucked valuable time away from me. I also felt embarrassed because all of my friends and family were waiting for these wonderful life events to happen for me, and they never did. I felt so terrible at the time; I was completely stunned and had to grieve the loss of my dreams that never came true. I remember thinking, how on earth am I going to tell people what happened?

The *narcissists tend to set you up for a big disappointment, many get off on causing you pain and making your life more difficult.* Looking for patterns in both relationships, there were always great promises prior to important events in my life, and then both Miguel and Kyle would always do something right before or after the event to ruin it for me. Reflect back on your birthdays, holidays, and work accomplishments, did your dysfunctional partner do things to sabotage those days for you?

If this has happened to you or it continues to happen, I understand how upsetting and disappointing this is, it's the worst. However, you can still enjoy life and accomplish what you need to get done. Healthy thinking after this happens and support helps to prevent a bad situation from becoming worse. Sometimes you need to take a big deep breath and push yourself to get things done. One way to take your power back is to achieve things on your own despite your dysfunctional partner's efforts to tear you down. This is especially satisfying if you were told that you needed them or could not do things on your own. You do not need toxic people in your life and you can do a lot all by yourself.

Looking back at my childhood for clues, I have made some meaningful connections to help me deal with future-faking. My parents, especially my mother, from a very early age, made it clear that I would feel happy and complete once I was married and had children. They also made it clear that there were so many emotions that I did not understand because I wasn't a mother. These comments were unintentionally very hurtful. My parents were very proud of my academic and professional achievements but it was obvious that they felt something was missing in my unmarried adult life. This is not so unusual as I have heard that my other single friends' parents also do this. When my two toxic relationships ended I felt that I disappointed my parents.

I believe that *I was so impacted by future-faking because not only did I have to let go of my dreams, but also my parents' dreams for me. I needed to have another look at my beliefs around happiness in adult life and I needed to rethink my ideas.* I created a new belief, I did not need to have a spouse or children to live a meaningful life. If you are like me and have always been in a relationship, it can be hard to believe that you can find happiness alone. You can! You need to work on changing your thinking and be mindful of all the things that bring you joy in life. You are the only person that can complete you and make you happy.

Now, putting on my psychologist hat, I would tell you that it is essential to mourn these losses. You still have to get up out of bed in the morning, go to work, and pay your bills. If you do not do these things, life will get worse, not better. That being said please cry, feel sad, talk about the confusion, anger and sadness with your friends, family and your therapist. All of these things are necessary to close this chapter in your life. My suggestion to you is to find a healthy balance of trying to be a functional human being and processing grief and healing. I know this is so hard and if you need to take a day and stay in bed and cry, that's okay; make it a day, not a month.

When a loved one makes promises and breaks them and abandons us out of the blue it hurts and is very sad.

Don't hold the emotions of grief in. *Grief is not a linear process. Sometimes you take two steps forward and two steps back, and that is okay.* Be kind and patient with yourself. Believing a "future faker" is not your fault. The Cluster B personality type will stoop very low to manipulate you and to get what they need from you, and this means playing on your hopes and dreams. They are very good con artists and liars and rarely stop to consider that their games are hurting you.

It may take some time, but after you get through the grieving step, I promise that you will eventually be able to sit back and say, "Thank God those future plans didn't happen!" "Thank God I did not waste another day of my precious life with that person!" Being married to, raising children with, managing money, building a home with and doing any other future plans with a Cluster B person is gruelling, difficult, painful, and emotionally torturous. When the wound is fresh, it is hard to see that your life can be so much better without them, but it will be! It may help to be honest with yourself and think back about whether the relationship was ever really that good.

I thought my relationship with Kyle was pretty awesome but, considering his chronic cheating and lies, it really wasn't that great, ever. I also had to accept that I never really knew Kyle, our relationship was mostly an illusion, and to him, just a game. It is tough to accept that what was special and true in your mind didn't matter to them. Kyle, who at one time I considered to be the nicest guy I ever met, ended up threatening to have me arrested and to ruin my career, and smeared my reputation all to keep his dark identity a secret and to intimidate me to stay quiet.

I thought my relationship with Miguel would be fabulous one day, but looking back it was obviously his future-faking that had me believe that, because things were never fabulous, to begin with. Sometimes, being brutally honest about our relationships is painful, but it will help you to move on and learn from your mistakes. Sometimes you need to rip off the bandaid and see things for what they really were.

REFLECTION POINTS

- How do you feel about the concept of future-faking? Does it resonate with you?
- How mindful are you?
- Is there work to be done to help you be present and enjoy life from moment to moment?
- What is happening in your life right now, that you value?
- What 5 things can you be grateful for right now?
- Do you feel there is anything for you to grieve about your existing or previous relationship?
- What childhood belief systems about your future or adult life do you need to change or modify?

PART 3

"...that's the thing about narcissists. They can try to fool you, with all their heart, but in the end, they're just fooling themselves."

—ELLIE FOX

Chapter 9

It's not me - It's definitely You!

I HAVE CARRIED OUT my own research over the years, by talking to fellow survivors of narcissistic relationships and reading books and peer-reviewed articles. My findings have shown that gaslighting, projections, character assassination, or smearing, for the purposes of manipulation and control; are some of the more common tools used by Cluster B personality types, especially by narcissists.

Most people have heard of gaslighting. According to Relate, the relationship counselling organisation, *gaslighting refers to the practice of trying to convince someone they're wrong about something even when they aren't.* Many of us are guilty of a little gaslighting, especially when we do not want to be proven wrong, or we refuse to hear what our partner has to say, even if they might be right. This is a form of being petty; however, when a narcissistic partner engages in gaslighting behaviour the outcome can be far more dangerous.

In my case gaslighting became another form of abuse. It was done repeatedly over a long period of time, with vicious intent to make me doubt myself and lose confidence in my own beliefs. Gaslighting has been known to make people question their own sanity, their own intuition and erode their self-esteem. I was constantly and deliberately subjected to gaslighting in this way.

Another common behaviour that shows up in narcissistic relationships is the use of projections. When the controlling partner begins to feel bad or experience unwanted thoughts and emotions, they project their thoughts and feelings onto their partner. This way they no longer have to feel them and can make their partner the 'bad' person, rather than feeling bad about themselves.

The problem with projecting feelings in this way is that the abusive partner can only find temporary relief from their emotional or mental pain and so continues to project and very soon this becomes a destructive habit, often used as a way of manipulating or controlling a partner, causing a great deal of pain in the process.

The outcome of this behaviour in my own experience was feeling confused and betrayed. Always being made to feel as though everything I did and said was wrong or bad was exhausting. I became very frustrated as a result of this constant attack on my character, and over time, even questioned my own values and qualities. It is very frustrating when your partner accuses you of things that you aren't doing. I felt like I was always second-guessing myself.

So, after experiencing gaslighting and projections on a regular basis, by far the most damaging attack I ever experienced was the smearing of my reputation. The toxic partner has everything to gain by making you look bad. One of their biggest fears is exposure and others finding out what is behind their mask. To avoid this, they will proactively try to make you look crazy, abusive or violent to gain credibility. If you uncover their deception and lies, prepare yourself to be attacked even more.

Reflecting on my own personal story, Miguel used gaslighting and projections to manipulate, control and abuse me emotionally.

I don't recall any smearing from Miguel; my theory is that Miguel was so concerned with putting out a great image for himself and his life, that it wouldn't have suited him to besmirch my character. If I was violent, crazy, or had some major defect, in Miguel's mind he would probably look foolish for staying with me for five years.

When I found out about Miguel cheating, he used gaslighting to blame me for the affair. Miguel said I made it too easy for him to cheat because I was too nice, I didn't ask enough questions and I was responsible since I gave him so much trust and kindness. He positioned his cheating as a way he could receive the excessive amounts of love he craved. Miguel also said I finished school before him and had more time to date, and he worked so hard during medical school and residency he felt entitled to have fun. Miguel blamed me for not understanding this because I, of course, did not go to medical school.

The extent to which Miguel tried to convince me that the affair was my fault was infuriating. I never believed this and found it insulting, but Miguel put up a valiant effort trying to convince me that he had to cheat because I was too nice and trusting. In his eyes, he was the victim. Somehow it was my fault for not understanding how hard he worked over the years and how he deserved to have flings. Miguel tried to turn it around and make it sound like I was the selfish one.

One day, due to our conflicting work schedules, Miguel had worked the night shift and I wasn't going to see him until later that day. We talked on the phone in the morning after I had left for work and he confirmed that he was home and going to eat and get some sleep before heading back into work. I discovered he hadn't gone home that morning, because I had left breakfast out for him and when I got home, it was still there. The bed was still made and

Miguel never made the bed. Add to this the fact that our leaky shower was still very dry. Miguel would never go to work without showering. I knew it was highly unlikely that he had been home that day at all.

When asked about this, Miguel became furious and said I was crazy. I was accused of being a crazy detective and snooping around looking for problems to complain about. Miguel said he wished he had a normal girlfriend and not a paranoid one looking for water drops in the shower. He avoided explaining his whereabouts that day and in fact, didn't talk to me for three days. When he finally decided to talk four days later, he blamed his silent treatment on me for asking such silly questions. This was one of his textbook gaslighting moments. So where did he go after his shift that day? I have no clue. I'm guessing a nurse's house. I let the issue go because his behaviour after I confronted him was so harsh.

Miguel also abused me financially by projecting his economic distress onto me. During his residency, Miguel borrowed tens of thousands of pounds from me. I co-signed for him to finance a car, I paid for flights and trips, and I even added him as a cardholder to my credit card accounts. When his parents would come to visit, I would spend my days with them and pay for their meals and our outings together. I also bought Miguel clothes and would finance the maintenance of our home. If a friend got married I would be the one who bought the gift, with my money. Surprisingly, Miguel liked to call me cheap every chance he could. He also liked to criticise me for being irresponsible with money when I had excellent credit and no debt. Miguel expected me to share my money with him but his money was his. This was his way of manipulating me into giving him money when he wanted it.

When Miguel started to make money as a doctor, he didn't step up to his financial responsibilities. He did, however, start to buy himself more expensive clothes and take more expensive trips.

Miguel was never able to see things from my point of view; he lacked empathy for the financial burden I was carrying, and asking him to take more financial responsibility for our life together would result in a screaming match followed by the typical silent treatment for a few days. Even though it was frustrating and unfair, I always gave in and ended up agreeing with Miguel, in the hope that I would avoid the pending punishment that I had unfortunately become accustomed to.

Moving on to Kyle, in previous chapters I have talked about how Kyle, who cheated, lied and stole, would like to claim to be the moral one in our relationship. Kyle had an addiction to pornography, sex, alcohol and nicotine. I live my life with the intention of being a decent human being and treating others with kindness. I also don't drink, smoke, or even curse. I don't consider myself perfect, I do suffer from a mild shoe addiction! However going back to a serious note, Kyle genuinely made me question how I could improve my values and morals. He made me feel like maybe I wasn't really a good person.

It is possible that the inner conflict and turmoil that Kyle was dealing with as a result of growing up with certain values, but living the opposite of many of these values, may have created a sense of conflict. As a result, Kyle would go out of his way to make me feel as though I was amoral, a bad person and someone whose life values were not centred around being a good person.

Kyle was a covert difficult person; once again, he liked to attack me in very subtle ways. He used nice words and what appeared to be genuine concern about my soul to confuse and manipulate me.

Now, looking back, it is pretty clear Kyle was projecting his own character flaws and lack of moral compass onto me, resulting in my feeling attacked emotionally and as though I wasn't enough. When he wasn't doing that I think he was just trying to see if he could get me to question myself or my sanity in some way.

Kyle would often gaslight me during the last year of our relationship, making me question whether I was needy or demanding. The interesting thing was, Kyle never wanted to be alone. Needing alone time was simply a ruse that he used so he could spend time with other women. I found out later on that he used the excuse of 'needing alone time' with the other ladies he was seeing too. This is one thing that Kyle and Miguel shared in common, they could not ever be alone.

Kyle also told hurtful lies about me to other women. During our relationship, he would compliment me excessively on how much he enjoyed the way I rubbed his back, cooked for him, bought him clothing or thoughtful gifts and how smart he thought I was. He told other women the exact opposite. He told his other lovers that I was pretty dumb, the worst cook, never rubbed his back or bought him nice gifts. Uncovering these truths, I felt embarrassed and extremely hurt. How could someone provide me with so much flattery and compliments in person and then go behind my back and badmouth me in this way? No normal adult says these things about their partners. Of course, the answer is that in order for him to maintain these relationships, he made sure that all of the women pitied him and wanted to save him from his loveless relationship with me.

Okay, so now, after you have lived through gaslighting, projections and smear campaigns, what do you do to recover? An important note to keep in mind is that you need to be extremely cautious with these individuals, because many will do anything to preserve their ego and image, and many will never back down from any kind of confrontation or perceived attack. Getting even is not a part of recovery. Remember, while they probably know right from wrong, most lack remorse, empathy, or any form of kindness or compassion. Also, perspective-taking is not a strength of theirs. They are all about themselves, their needs and whatever it takes to get what they want, when they want it, regardless of who it hurts.

After gaslighting, projections and smear campaigns, it's normal to feel anxious and depressed. With work, the right intentions and plenty of healing, you will recover. Make a list of affirmations about who you are and say them out loud. Do something nice for yourself. Practice mindfulness and self-care. You are a wonderful person who deserves healthy love. You did nothing to deserve or warrant your partner treating you in this way. Many people in your life know and value who you are. Don't give your abuser the power to ruin your self-image or self-worth.

Looking back at my childhood I never really observed any forms of gaslighting, projections, or smearing in my home. My parents were usually pretty honest about their complaints that they had and maybe at times their reactions were exaggerated, but I can't recall any clear examples of the above themes of this chapter. If I was ever caught saying something untrue about someone, my parents would make me apologise to that person. Lying was not acceptable in my home. My parents would argue but they would never badmouth each other to their kids.

The only personal connection that I can make is that I would never do any of these things. I usually accept too much blame in situations where I have little fault, which isn't good either. I struggle to understand how people could engage in behaviour that I consider unacceptable. I tend to want to see the good in people and brush over the bad and believe that people in my world will do the right thing. At times I can be naive and overly trusting. When I finally make the connection that someone has taken advantage of me or hurt me, it takes me a long time to wrap my head around what just happened due to these factors.

REFLECTION POINTS

- What examples of gaslighting, projections and smearing can you identify in your relationship either presently or with an ex?
- How did those techniques make you feel in the moment and how did you react?
- Why do you think you reacted the way you did and how will you react next time?
- What do you take responsibility for in your relationship that perhaps you shouldn't?
- Is there anything you need to forgive yourself for?

Chapter 10

Once a Cheat...

WITHIN THE CLUSTER B personality group, narcissists tend to be known for promiscuity and infidelity. Following my personal research and having spoken to fellow survivors, this seems to be a consistent and common toxic trait. To be honest, I have never heard of a case of a narcissist being completely faithful. So, what is it about them that makes them cheat?

While I have a few of my own theories, *what you actually need to know is that your partner's infidelity is all about them, their choices and their need to feed their supply.* Being unfaithful is a conscious decision that someone makes, regardless of your actions or anyone else's. Now, keep in mind that not all people who cheat have a Cluster B personality disorder - there are lots of reasons for infidelity. The difference between a mistake, or complicated entanglement and a narcissistic cheater is quite clear, so let's dive into my theory.

In my opinion, there are two types of cheats. The first is someone who makes a mistake, is emotionally immature or who lacks the communication skills to leave a relationship honestly. These are the people who feel terrible about cheating and then stop because they realise it was a terrible mistake. The second cheats to meet their personal needs. They tend to have no intention of leaving their main relationship, are intentional about infidelity and are not interested in developing emotional maturity. These cheaters are the ones who think the grass is always greener on the other side but want to still keep their lawn too!

These individuals seek excitement and new supply and do not find comfort in the stability of a relationship. They like to deceive others and feel like they are getting away with something. The narcissist loves to engage in risk-taking and reckless behaviour. They also lack empathy and do not care about the damage cheating does to others. They struggle with intimacy and do not experience true human connections that love and intimacy bring. They can act as if they are in love, but they usually do not seek intimacy or the give and take that a true love connection forms.

Sex is just another way of them gaining the attention they crave along with meeting physical and sometimes manipulation needs. In many cases to them, sex is probably as meaningful as eating a ham sandwich for lunch. Also, to a narcissist, a partner is just another object, almost like another garment, that makes them look and feel good. The relationship and sex are never about the two of you; depending on the degree of narcissism you are dealing with, it is usually about their needs, image, and feelings.

Cheating is a symptom of their pathology. There is no point in asking yourself why they did it to you. Know it has nothing to do with you. Know that this behaviour has probably been going on for years and probably won't ever stop. I doubt you are the first person they ever betrayed. In my opinion, going to therapy will not help the narcissist to stop cheating.

I was going to therapy with Kyle because he had confessed to cheating with a woman early on in the relationship and wanted to come clean so we could move forward in an honest way. Kyle never stopped cheating with the other woman. He cheated with her throughout our entire relationship and with 10 others. He even went to therapy with some of the other women too! One partner is never enough for these personalities, and in order to avoid abandonment, a diminished supply of attention or praise, they will employ whatever tactics are necessary to keep as many people as they want or need in their lives.

As mentioned earlier, Cluster B personalities are very difficult to treat; to the extent that many therapists will refuse to work with them. There is no medicine to cure these disorders and the progress they make in therapy can be very minimal. For your own physical and emotional safety, if your toxic partner is cheating, it is better to cut your losses and get out. It is a sign of disrespect and complete disregard for your physical and emotional wellbeing. In my opinion, you can never trust a habitual cheater. I understand that when you are deep into a relationship, especially if you have children, leaving is always easier said than done. I understand the desire to want to fight and save your relationship. I own up to giving Kyle a second chance after he confessed to cheating.

How could I not give Kyle a second chance? He was so nice and sweet. He said it was just a few times when he was drunk when we first started dating. Kyle made it seem like this wasn't even cheating but, due to his high morals, he didn't want to bring past sin into a new relationship. He also confessed that he only had sex with this other woman because he felt so inferior to me that when he was drunk, he wanted to be with someone he felt superior to (he is not superior to this other woman either!)

Kyle "cried," said he felt so ashamed, and that he was so sorry that he hurt a daughter of God. Then, after this confession, he fell asleep and took a nap. I was stunned and didn't know what to think. This confession was just so odd. I consulted with family and friends about what to do. This was so painful because Kyle knew the Miguel cheating story and I had made it very clear that I would struggle to cope if this happened to me again. I really didn't think I could live through infidelity twice in a row and I couldn't help but wonder how Kyle 'Mr. Moral' could end up being a cheater.

I did things differently with Kyle because I wanted to believe that he was different. I think that I had some abandonment issues after Miguel, and I didn't want another public failure. I didn't want to have to tell everyone another relationship ended because of cheating. *I was convinced that people were going to start to think that there was something wrong with me.* So, I made a list of Kyle's good and bad qualities and there were just so many good ones. I decided that I had the energy and was willing to go through therapy and forgive Kyle. I would ask myself, "Where am I ever going to find such a great guy like him?" Needless to say, I was very wrong. He told me and the therapist that his affair was long over and he wanted me to trust him and for us to be together. Of course, these were all lies combined with future-faking.

Toward the end of our relationship, Kyle said some things that I really should have paid attention to. He asked my thoughts on his brother's open relationship. He told me that his brother and his brother's girlfriend went to a swingers' club and that it helped his brother - *who, I believe, also has Cluster B personality traits and is a known cheater* - to no longer want to cheat on his girlfriend. Kyle would also talk about guys at work who always used to cheat on their wives and eventually stopped, to see how I would react.

My reactions to these stories were always disgust. Kyle would always ask me when he would work late or have to go anywhere overnight if I was being a "good girl." I heard he used this line with the other women too. Here is your next tip: it is common for cheaters to suspect their partners of doing the same things they are guilty of - projection. If you are ever accused of cheating in any way, shape or form, out of the blue, this is a red flag.

Though the Miguel situation was different, there were some similarities with my second narcissist. Miguel and Kyle each confessed to one cheating incident. I caught Kyle in others years later. Both blamed cheating on alcohol. Substance abuse and some Cluster B disorders go hand in hand, but being drunk is not a justification for cheating, nor is being an addict.

Miguel swore he only cheated *once* in his whole life, and that he couldn't believe the girl got pregnant that one and only time - I don't believe this either -. Since Miguel is much more grandiose, his confession involved sobbing and throwing his body to the floor, him getting down on his hands and knees begging for forgiveness. In typical self-absorbed fashion, Miguel also said that he didn't know why these terrible things always happened to him. Looking back now, I guess the comment really isn't so bizarre because, in the eyes of the narcissist, they are always the victim.

When I originally found Miguel's passport I knew he was lying and I knew he was travelling places, but I had no clue there was a pregnant girl. When I found out about the unborn child, I totally dissociated from what I was being told and felt like I was outside of my own body in a fog. That night I didn't cry or scream. I walked up to the guest bedroom and locked the door and went to sleep. Types of dissociative and "freezing" behaviours are forms of my maladaptive coping skills. Ever since I was a small child this has been how I have responded to fear, threat, danger, anything upsetting, and punishment. My knee jerk reaction is never to fight and never to flee, it's to freeze. I am at my calmest when there is interpersonal chaos in my world because I block it all out. That night I was not able to talk or scream. I think it was amazing that I wandered up the stairs and went to sleep. I felt nothing. I was numb, disconnected from reality.

I still talk to my therapist about dissociating from my feelings and even struggled to make progress when doing Eye Movement Desensitisation and Reprocessing - EMDR - for trauma because of my difficulty with feeling negative emotions. I love to feel happy emotions but really ignore the negative ones. If something feels bad, scary, or painful I choose not to feel it. This is why I ignore my intuition too. This is quite common and maybe you also have this poor coping skill. Don't worry, you can change it! I think my tendency to dissociate from the bad stuff and freeze also aided me in ignoring red flags and made me an easy person to lie to.

I just believed almost everything Kyle and Miguel told me. Miguel even told me that his globe-trotting and cheating was my fault because I was too nice and never asked questions. I bought a house and moved out as soon as I could after finding out about the pregnant French woman. I didn't want to go to therapy and try to work it out. I wanted to get away. After I heard the truth, I froze, then I engaged in another basic survival skill which I rarely apply - I fled.

As someone working in mental health, I can tell you it is important to feel negative emotions. They serve a purpose and help us to protect ourselves and know what not to do in the future. Here is an example where I say those that cannot do, teach! I have made progress with being more connected to my emotions, but it is a struggle for me. If you are sad, anxious or angry, sit with that feeling, be patient and kind to yourself and process it. Make a habit of practising self-talk after an argument or other unpleasant event; ask yourself what you are feeling, and why. Don't push that feeling away: welcome it.

Now, reflecting on my narcissists, I think even I knew deep down that Miguel was a likely cheater because of his overt womanising behaviours and open love for sex and pornography. No one thought in a million years that Kyle would be a cheater: he just seemed to love me so much. I later found out that he had a secret pornography addiction too. The bottom line is that both of my narcissistic lovers were cheaters, both had unprotected sex with other women, I'm guessing they both drastically played down the number of women they had slept with, and neither had any genuine remorse about it.

Like I said previously, the second time I caught Kyle cheating and confronted him, he laughed. He bit his lip, trying to hold it in because he knew that laughing in that situation was wrong, but he just could not stop himself. He told me that he was sick and that he had tried to tell me multiple times that he was screwed up. Kyle indirectly tried to make me think he somehow warned me about these 10 other affairs. Miguel's over the top fake apology and remorse was his way of trying to keep me in his life, probably eventually moving me over to the side piece category. I put these examples here to reconfirm how selfish and narcissistic these men were.

Looking back over my life for any other connections to infidelity, I can honestly say that I never knew of any men or women in my family who were cheaters. I didn't see it in my community much either. Almost all my friends' parents were married, as was almost everyone in my family. Cheating was not part of my framework for romantic relationships. Deep down, I honestly didn't expect a partner in a serious relationship to cheat because I had never seen it growing up. I had my doubts about Miguel but thought that there was no way he would actually do that. Who *would* do that?

Here is a tip I needed to learn: just because you would never do something, that doesn't mean other people operate by your moral code. Also, no matter how nice, good, helpful, kind, smart, or pretty you are to your partner, that will not keep them faithful.

What I can apply from my childhood experiences and part of my personality is that sometimes I avoid things because if I recognise it, I have to do something about it, and that is painful. This is simply called being in denial. I don't want to think that people I love would hurt me. I want to believe that they will always do right by me. Ignorance is bliss and, sometimes, we think we are protecting ourselves by living in the dark. Unfortunately, we are only hurting ourselves. What we don't know can and will hurt us. Looking the other way, freezing and dissociating are all ways to stay in denial temporarily and give you some time before you actually have to act. I have worked very hard at improving these maladaptive coping skills, so I can tell you that they can be changed.

So, how do you recover when someone you love and trust betrays you in this way? How do you trust another partner? How do you want to ever be with another partner? I think the answers to these questions are different for everyone. I can give you my best shot of helping with some tips and things to consider.

Tips on Infidelity

First, not everyone cheats. There are committed and faithful individuals in this world. Just because this happened to you, it doesn't mean it will happen again. I know this is a hard one to see after you have been hurt but it is true.

If something doesn't feel right, say something immediately. Don't be afraid to ask questions.

Don't just pay attention to words, make sure the words match the behaviours.

Know your self-worth and don't tolerate cheating. Do not take any responsibility for your toxic partner's cheating behaviours. This is always their fault.

Turn to what helps you to heal; this could be spirituality, meditation, therapy, journaling, travel, exercise, or speaking with friends. You need to talk everything through, so process your pain with people you trust.

Be patient and kind to yourself. Don't jump into another relationship too soon, or you run the risk of projecting some of your old relationship pains onto your new partner.

One of my best fellow psychologist friends gives this advice to her sons: "Be happy with who you are, put yourself first and then you can invite someone in to share your life with you."

If you are just getting out of a toxic relationship, you have work to do first before you can invite someone in to share your happiness and life.

It is important to accept that trust may be something that you struggle with after infidelity. That's fine and expected. Time also helps with this, so be patient.

Here is another question you may be asking yourself: *should I tell the other woman? Should I warn her, should I tell her to leave me and my family alone? Should I rat out the narcissist so he learns his lesson?* The narcissist will never learn their lesson because they have no conscience and no ability to feel bad about their behaviour. If you are looking to punish or teach a lesson to a narcissist, the odds are that you are wasting time and energy that can be better put toward your recovery.

You may feel compelled to reach out to the other woman or man to try to save your relationship, make the behaviour stop, or to warn them. This may be a way that you seek justice for yourself, too. I will tell you what I did in each case.

With Miguel, I made no attempt to discover the identity of the pregnant woman, and therefore no attempt to contact her. I didn't ask Miguel her name or any specific details about her. Keep in mind, Miguel was my explosive narcissist and I was probably still scared of making him angry and getting punished. Once you discover cheating you also may start to wonder what else they are capable of.

It is important to note that, unfortunately, some Cluster B personalities can be violent and dangerous. Therefore, more often than not, it's better to not provoke them. If I am honest with myself, after I discovered what happened, I wish I'd had the guts to warn the pregnant French woman, to tell her the truth, but I didn't. I think that after I got out of my relationship with Miguel I felt weak and angry at myself for tolerating his nonsense. I knew that I wanted to stand up for myself and be tougher in the future.

When I found out about Kyle's cheating, I did contact the other woman. She didn't respond, but in the moment it felt good for me to know that I didn't back down and that I was able to stand up for myself and do what I thought was right. Like I said previously, that relationship continued behind my back, so my contacting her didn't stop anything. I should have just ended things with Kyle once I found out about the cheating. As you read you will get the picture that I am pretty open and honest about my mistakes. Sometimes in these situations, we react emotionally and not logically. If I could do things over, I would have just ended things with Kyle and not reached out to the woman. Looking back on the situation with

Miguel, it was probably a good idea to never contact the pregnant lady.

So after these two relationships that were plagued with deceit and cheating how did I feel? Well, I felt terrible for a few hours after I discovered the cheating and then I did what I always used to do, I tried to focus on the positive and not feel anything. Years after Miguel and when things finally ended with Kyle I took the time to really process all of those emotions and pain that those infidelities and lies caused. It was really tough because I was trying to deal with so many betrayals from two people at once. This is the risk you run when you do not process pain and feel your emotions; sooner or later all of that yuck will come up, and when it comes up at the same time it is emotionally draining. I felt sad, stupid, anxious, angry, and basically any other negative emotion you could imagine. This time I knew it was too risky to push the feelings aside and I had to suck it up and feel all those painful emotions.

My friends and family were exceptionally great to me during this time. I went to stay with friends in London, went on multiple beach getaways with the girls, stayed with my parents for a while, and had lots of visitors and phone calls. I talked and talked about how I felt and they never got tired of listening. I think if I would have really taken the time to feel and learn from my relationship with Miguel, I would have never gotten involved with Kyle. Sometimes looking back on all the stuff I put up with I become angry with myself and say, "What on Earth were you thinking?" Honestly, I know now what I was thinking and why and I hope I apply that knowledge in the future to avoid toxic men. I try to show myself compassion and forgiveness and focus on making better choices in the future.

Red Flags:

- Hiding phones, leaving their phones in the car, constantly checking their phones or not checking their phone when it rang
- No social media or fake social media accounts
- Making up stories about crazy dangerous exs to keep you from contacting other partners
- Sudden, new interests or hanging out with new friends
- Wearing new clothes and lying about where they came from
- All of a sudden working extra shifts or working late, going into work early
- Delay in responding to calls or messages
- Coming home with "new sexual positions" or wanting to try new things sexually
- Sudden excessive interest in sex or a sudden lack of interest in sex

REFLECTION POINTS

- How do you feel about infidelity?
- How can you reshape any negative self-talk?
- What message did you observe about infidelity growing up?
- How have you applied that message to your relationships?
- List the red flags that you noticed that made you question your partner's faithfulness.
- Did you have a gut feeling that they were cheating?
- How can you become more aware of your intuition and act on it?
- If you were your best friend or therapist, what would you tell yourself about infidelity in relationships?
- What advice would you give a friend in the same situation?

Chapter 11

The Terrible Twos

YOU MAY FEEL SOME compassion for narcissists who have had a rough childhood, suffered abuse, neglect, or some other trauma, which they will often tell you about within minutes of meeting them. Many do have significant abuse and neglect in their past. The irony is that these people were often very challenging children to raise, and often see themselves as victims when they were often offenders. They will tell stories of being abused, neglected or mistreated when that wasn't the case. The truth is if you dig a little deeper, you may discover that they were disobedient, anti-authority and entitled even as small children. There is a difference between children who were victims of abuse, neglected by parents and grew up in difficult circumstances. These individuals probably will have some emotional baggage from those experiences.

The truth is that not everyone who grows up experiencing any or all of these events is a narcissist. An explanation for bad behaviour is not a justification for bad behaviour. Everyone has hurt in their lives and most people are able to regulate their impulses and emotions as adults rather well. One of the wonderful things about being an adult is that you can decide to take care of your childhood wounds and self-improve. Some people with severe histories of abuse and neglect may have a harder time healing than others, but it is still possible.

It is interesting then to find that many Cluster B individuals, especially narcissists, go on to have very successful careers but not successful relationships. They often do well in school, hold the highest positions in professional jobs and are able to carry out high-level cognitive tasks. While they may not have the emotional maturity, they certainly have the intelligence needed to navigate the world. Also, they are willing to step on anyone to get what they want. Cheating, lying and hurting others to get ahead is in their DNA, literally. Sadly these qualities will get a person ahead in many professions, especially in the business world.

Emotional Immaturity

Many narcissists are emotionally immature; behaving as if stuck in their childhoods. They behave, love, and process emotions like small children or teenagers. You can see this in many ways, some of which we have discussed in previous chapters. As someone who works much more with small children than adults, I can tell you that little kids tend to be very selfish and egocentric. Developmentally, toddlers rely on others to meet their needs constantly and that is what they expect to happen. Little kids have to be taught and learn that they won't always get their way in life and that kicking, screaming, and throwing themselves on the floor is not an appropriate response to hearing the word "no".

Children are more sensitive and their feelings tend to get hurt rather easily. Oftentimes, for children and narcissists, emotional responses are somewhat intense in relation to the original offence. This manifests with both negative and positive emotions; for example, over the top laughter and demonstrations of joy for very simple pleasures.

If you have children, spend a lot of time around them or work with them you know that toddlers tend to be very emotionally needy. This is developmentally appropriate for a small child. They look for hugs, kisses, and constant company to make them feel secure, loved, and safe. Toddlers frequently want to physically attach themselves to their primary caregivers because they know that they need them for survival. The thought of being abandoned by a primary caregiver, even for a few hours, is often too much for a toddler to bear.

Due to their fragile egos, *narcissists also fear abandonment and need others for validation.* Like toddlers, they struggle to be alone. They need constant affection, praise, and attention. Like toddlers, they are not very good at entertaining themselves. Also, like small children, they get bored very easily. They are always on the lookout for new and exciting toys. Plus, they struggle to understand healthy boundaries.

Object Consistency

Another way that these toxic individuals share a commonality with very young and immature children is in the area of object consistency. Object consistency means knowing that a person, relationship, or concept exists even when you cannot see it. Very young children cry and become very upset when their caregivers leave the room or if they have to put a favourite toy down. They need to learn that even though they cannot see or touch something, it does not mean that the object does not exist or is gone forever. Many narcissists and other toxic individuals really struggle with this concept. Think about when you are in the shower and you dry off to see forty missed calls on your phone in twenty minutes. Your partner is upset because they wanted to get a hold of you and did not know where you were. Emotionally stable adults rarely engage in this kind of behaviour which is driven by panic and a sense of abandonment.

The narcissist only thinks they wanted to talk to you and you were not there, so they freak out.

Here is another area where object consistency is relevant in relationships where there is narcissistic abuse. Cheating and infidelity! Out of sight out of mind is a slogan that many narcissists operate by in relationships; if they are not physically in your presence, their relationship and commitment to you disappear too. This makes flirting and cheating easy for them. A lack of object consistency and a lack of remorse makes it nearly impossible for a partner to be faithful. Keep this in mind if your partner chronically cheats on you; as I stated in other chapters, this behaviour is very unlikely to stop.

Narcissism and Mental Health Disorders

Narcissistic, Borderline, Histrionic, and Antisocial personalities must have things their way. If they don't get their way, they tend not to take it so well. They may scream, throw a tantrum, refuse to talk, or act very irrationally if they cannot have what they want, or just take what they want and get their needs met no matter the cost of injury to others.

People with schizophrenia who hallucinate, experience extreme paranoia and struggle to separate realms of reality, can sometimes find it difficult to identify right from wrong or understand the consequences of their actions; this is very sad. Someone who struggles with bipolar disorder may also make poor decisions during a manic episode, struggling to control impulses and experiencing hallucinations and psychotic breaks, which again, is also very sad. These two disorders involve brain chemistry and therefore these disorders respond to medications.

There is no medication that treats Cluster B personality disorders or narcissism because their behaviours are not directly related to brain chemistry. People with this personality type know, and can choose, how to act. They decide not to do the right thing while many people with other mental health disorders have little control over their behaviours.

Another way that the narcissist is emotionally immature is in their black and white thinking. These dysfunctional people usually view others in their lives as either all good or all bad. When they are idealising you, the narcissist may struggle to see any of your flaws, but when they are upset with you they will only see you with negative eyes and even as a potential threat to them. They are incapable of being angry with a partner and also recognising that their loved one has good qualities at the same time.

Miguel & Kyle

I'll share some examples of displays of emotional immaturity from my two ex narcissist lovers. There are so many that I could write a book just with examples on this topic, but let's start with the overt, Miguel. Miguel had more tantrums than any two-year-old I have ever met. When any of his basic needs were not met, Miguel would tantrum. If he was hot, hungry, tired, or cold and I didn't fix it for him, he would tantrum. God forbid he had a sore throat or something more severe that I could not take away; then it would be a real explosion. Miguel could not take criticism of any kind or stand it if someone had a different opinion. If this happened, he would scream, yell, or storm out of the room. Miguel also did not care if I was sick, tired, or had something to do; if he wanted or needed something, he expected it right away. One time on a weekend trip to London, Miguel froze and stomped his feet in the middle of a busy intersection because I suggested he eat a muffin for breakfast and he did not want a muffin. He was 30 years old at the time.

Kyle, my covert narcissist, did not take criticism very well either; he would become visibly uncomfortable, turning red in the face and act very embarrassed if he was ever corrected or criticised. Kyle was never a screamer or a stomper around me, but he showed his extreme sensitivity like a shy little boy. Kyle acted like a toddler in the way he clung and hung onto me. He needed constant reassurance and physical touch. Kyle also needed a parent figure to make his appointments for him, tell him he needed to take a shower, and that he could not wear his police uniform for 3 days in a row without washing it. Once while lying in bed Kyle even commented on how he wished I was his mother, - weird, I know. Kyle's sense of humour was also like a small child's, laughing at things that really were not funny. As a side note, Kyle also laughed at very inappropriate times such as when he found out that his grandmother had died and when I confronted him with tears in my eyes about his betrayals.

So let's keep the comparison going with narcissists in relationships. I'm sure once I started with the toddler analogy you could already reflect on numerous examples in your head. Narcissists tend to only care about their individual needs. They always put their own needs first; even when it may seem as if they are prioritising you. The give and take of normal relationships is something they tend to avoid. The concept of equanimity and fairness is usually out of their realm of reality and is often left to the people-pleaser in the relationship.

Healthy people, after they mature emotionally, mentally and physically, past their childhood and teen years, understand that in life you don't always get what you want and so they are able to accept that fact. I have also noticed that these partners have extreme reactions to other opinions, lifestyles, and just about any idea that they do not support or understand. Their way is always the best way. Reasoning and perspective-taking are usually major deficits for these dysfunctional people. Do not expect this to ever change!

We deserve so much more. Love is not supposed to be scary, unkind or disrespectful. Love should be giving and pure. Narcissists are incapable of providing true intimacy or forming healthy attachments with romantic partners. After dedicating time and effort to these relationships, it can be excruciating to have to accept this fact. The sooner you do, the easier it will be to recover. Once you recover and you look back, you will realise how unhealthy this kind of relationship was for you, and that's okay because when you look back you will have moved on and the relationship will no longer hold any power over you.

Looking back on my childhood, I was taught that being emotionally strong and tough were desirable traits. My parents did a good job of not reinforcing or tolerating bad behaviours in their children. Personally, *I think I maybe needed a softer touch at times growing up and to feel that my parents cared more when I was sad or hurt.* That isn't a criticism of them; everyone has different emotional needs and I think I needed more comforting and validation of my feelings as a child. I think since I didn't get it, I tried to give it to my partners. I was always placating, comforting, and caring for my partners' emotional needs and my emotional needs continued to go unmet. I needed to learn that my job was not to be their mothers.

Red flags of emotional immaturity:

- Toddler-like tantrums
- Sudden mood changes
- The expectation that their problems be fixed by their partner, akin to a mother-child relationship
- Inability to take any form of criticism
- Impatience
- Need to have everything their way

- Feeling that their needs, opinions, and beliefs are superior to others
- Displays of inappropriate emotions given the circumstance
- Overly affectionate, clingy or emotionally needy
- Black and white thinking
- Inability to engage in perspective-taking and reasoning

REFLECTION POINTS

- What kind of emotional stability do you expect or need from a partner?
- How would you describe your own current emotional state? Where do you want it to be and how will you get it there?
- List some examples of emotional immaturity that were displayed by your partner.
- How did their behaviours make you feel? How did you react to those behaviours?
- Why do you think you tolerated the displays of emotional immaturity by your partner?
- Do you have other loved ones who struggle with emotional immaturity? Can you see any patterns?
- How would you describe the examples of emotional maturity that you observed in your childhood caregivers?

PART 4

"Lies don't end relationships the truth does."
                    —SHANNON L. ALDER

CHAPTER 12

An Out of Body Experience

WHEN WE ARE STRESSED, feel threatened or are dealing with incredibly toxic situations we are likely to engage a maladaptive coping mechanism. In this chapter, we will explore three of the most common - amnesia, denial and dissociation.

AMNESIA

Amnesia is a maladaptive coping skill that contributes to staying in a toxic relationship. Unlike the typical memory loss that many of us understand amnesia to be, in this case, I am referring to the act of filtering out the bad and remembering only the good in our dysfunctional partners. There is a real danger in forgetting about the violence, cheating, abandonment, neglect, insults, and abuse.

When amnesia is active we ignore the mind's natural tendency to lean towards the negative and instead we overcompensate on recognising the positive. This was especially true for me after arguments. Like many survivors, I would pay more attention to the good in my partners and our relationships. I remember after one of Kyle's episodes a good friend who also is a counsellor told me that she hopes one day I could see how much Kyle put me through. I remember nodding my head and being respectful to my friend but thinking, "What is she talking about? Kyle is so good to me."

DISSOCIATION

Frequently throughout this book, I talk about my go-to maladaptive coping skill, dissociation. Dissociation is when you separate yourself from what is going on. It is similar to denial, but it is also a deep disconnect from your emotions. It is when the feeling hurts too much so you avoid feeling anything. If you ever felt like you were walking around in a fog after a painful event you may have been dissociating.

When I dissociate, *I feel completely disconnected from my body, almost as if I am standing outside of myself.* There are also different degrees to which you may dissociate; you may do this mildly after an insult or small argument and you may do so majorly after a more life-altering event, like a death or divorce. Why do we dissociate? We do this to protect ourselves in the moment but unfortunately, it is often very counterproductive.

Dissociation may make you feel better and may make it easier for you to carry about your day and get things done. Dissociating may help you to put a smile on your face and act like everything is normal. It also keeps you in a standstill, as the less you feel and recognise, the fewer decisions you have to make. The biggest plus to me dissociating in my two relationships was my ability to avoid feeling negative feelings such as rejection, humiliation, sadness, and anger. Unfortunately, that came at a steep price.

Pain and suffering teach us a whole slew of lessons. Emotional pain serves the same purpose as physical pain. If you touch something that is hot and you get burnt, cognitively you know not to touch it again and at the very least, to be extremely cautious around the flame. If you walk through a field with poison ivy and get terrible itchy red blisters, you know not to walk through that field again. The same principle applies to our emotions. We feel negative emotions for a reason. One of the reasons I think I stayed with Miguel and Kyle so long was because I wasn't paying attention and I wasn't mindful of what I was feeling and how they were treating me. If we don't feel anger, sadness, embarrassment, and all that other lousy stuff, we won't know who or what to stay away from either.

DENIAL

Another common maladaptive coping skill that I am guilty of using and I know is a common trait among abuse survivors is denial. Especially after the idealisation and love-bombing stages, we just don't want to admit that our partners are acting like such sick jerks. We love them and want to focus on the good. We decide not to see the bad traits and ignore them. We rationalise their behaviour or make excuses for them. We may even blame ourselves. This is very common in toxic relationships.

Denial also comes up when we are not ready to leave a relationship or make changes. Cognitive dissonance, those two drastic competing ideas about something, in my opinion really aids our denial. When you have the total opposite thoughts and beliefs about a person or an event it causes so much confusion. One day your partner is the prince and the next he is the frog, it doesn't help that everyone you know sees the prince and you only get to see the frog; these two competing ideas make it hard to see who they really are.

I know I was guilty, especially with Kyle, of saying I didn't see it or I didn't know mistreatment was going on. I didn't see everything or the degree of dysfunction until after the relationship was over but that is because I chose not to ask questions. I chose to ignore my intuition and inconsistencies in his stories that didn't add up. I didn't know things were as bad as they were but there were little signs along the way that I ignored, and I need to take responsibility for that. Now, I know I did this because after Miguel it was too much for me to think that Kyle was cut from the same cloth. Denial is another coping skill that gets us stuck. If we accept the truth, then we must do something about it and sometimes we don't want change or aren't ready for it. Again, here is where mindfulness can help. If you are truly practising mindfulness, ignoring what is going on in your environment is very difficult. Stay in the present and pay attention to all the behaviours you see. What do their words and actions show you?

REFLECTIONS

- When have you been in denial? How did you feel?
- Have you ever dissociated from a situation in your relationship? What could you have said to yourself to get unstuck?
- Do you suffer from amnesia in your relationships? What do you think about this? Does it resonate with you?

Chapter 13

Some Lovers <u>Are</u> Just For Christmas

ESTRANGEMENT AND DISCARDING SHOW up in many ways during these relationships. Personally, I think it is related to the very black and white thinking that these toxic individuals use to operate. They are either all in or completely checked out. When they are not completely checked out, they are looking for a way to check out.

Estrangement is related to discarding; when these dysfunctional people get tired of you or are offended by you, it is common for them to completely cut you off. Sometimes this is anticipated and sometimes it will come when you least expect it. Not only will they try to eliminate you from their lives, but they will also try to turn other people against you. They may try to turn your parents, siblings, best friends, neighbours and co-workers against you without feeling any remorse. Now sometimes the narcissist will cut people off permanently and sometimes they will hover around and come back.

People with traits of narcissism are known for holding a grudge. Forgiveness is certainly not a strong point for them, and the line between love and hate is a very fine one. In my personal experience, the severity of the estrangement or discarding is often dictated by the degree of the narcissistic injury that your partner feels. For example, if you call them out or catch them in lies, embarrass them in some way, or expose them to other people, odds are they will be out of your life very quickly. Remember that their egos are extremely fragile, and they can't handle looking bad in front of others. Now they may exit peacefully, and you may never hear from them again, or they may try to attack you in multiple ways because you figured out or exposed the truth.

In my experience, it is common for narcissists to have a history of struggling in a variety of close relationships. They may be estranged from their families or talk badly about loved ones. They may have a history of dramatically failed relationships. They may struggle to maintain friendships or have multiple conflicts at work. *They will almost always paint themselves as the victims* in these stories with the other characters being the lunatics who wronged them. Keep in mind it is healthy to remove toxic people from your life and not everyone should have a close relationship with their boss, neighbour, or mother, especially if they are abusive. It's good to ask questions and listen to the explanations carefully when your partner decides to completely cut someone out of their life or share a story about why they no longer see a loved one. Does the reason make sense to you? Are there any inconsistencies in their story?

Now discarding a romantic partner frequently happens because the narcissist has found someone new to toy with. It is not unusual for your partner to leave you and be living with his new supply the next day. I know, ouch! They probably will also flaunt and brag about their new supply on social media and to friends. This is incredibly shocking and hurtful and can be as emotionally raw as a death. They were with you yesterday and today they are gone and have a new life. When this happens it's natural and normal to have so many questions.

Now Miguel was connected to his family and would talk to them on the phone frequently and they would even come and stay with us for months at a time. I actually liked his parents and enjoyed spending time with them. Miguel wouldn't permanently cut family out of his life, but he would become very angry at his siblings, sister-in-law, and cousins, and get into intense verbal arguments with them followed by long periods of zero communication.

Miguel also liked to make people feel the estrangement and if he was at a family party with someone he was angry with, he would brag about how he ignored the estranged person or made him/her feel uncomfortable. If Miguel was ever questioned or criticised by any of his colleagues at work, he would become furious and completely ignore them. If you crossed Miguel he had no problem eliminating you from his life and trying his best to make you feel uncomfortable whenever he saw you.

After one of Kyle's breakdowns one October I reached out to one of his brothers to express that I was concerned about Kyle's drinking and mental health. His brother told me that Kyle really hadn't been around the family for the past four years. He told me that they invited him to gatherings and he rarely attended. Kyle would talk about feeling deep resentment towards his parents for homeschooling him. He also expressed feeling embarrassed by his siblings because he considered them to be learning disabled. Kyle seemed to be able to cut people out of his life as and when it suited him. After I finally discovered all of his lies and cheating, he disappeared; when the relationship finally ended I remember thinking I don't know this guy at all.

Looking back to some patterns from my childhood I saw a pretty significant history of estrangement in my family. After my grandparents died, my mother stopped talking to and seeing her siblings due to arguments over money. These arguments were heated screaming matches that contained below the belt insults and comments. Eventually, these arguments ended up in civil court where my grandparents' will was contested. No one was willing to see or consider the other's point of view. My grandfather was a janitor and my grandmother never worked so there wasn't really any money to fight over. This was very sad to me because my mother lost her parents and her only two siblings; all of a sudden it was like she had no family left, but this was her choice.

Not being loyal or doing something as bold as questioning what a family member did with 'the money' was something that would warrant getting completely cut off in my parents' eyes. I know similar situations happen in multiple families, and especially over money, but as I write this book my mother hasn't seen her brother or sister in 15 years, and I doubt she ever will. Even though my dad is a very nice guy, he tends to easily cut people out of his life if he feels he was wronged. My parents are not very forgiving people. I never really even thought too much about my parents no longer talking to my aunt and uncle until I casually mentioned it to a friend recently. My friend's response was, "I thought your parents were great, that's not normal." Then I started to think about those fights all those years ago and I realised that the events that happened after my grandparents died weren't healthy for anyone.

So how did I feel knowing that Miguel and Kyle were with new supplies and cheated and discarded me? When I finally took time to process it, I felt pretty awful. Especially reflecting on the pattern of idealisations and discards that I experienced with Kyle, I felt very foolish and angry. Like I said before, Kyle would wait to disappear right before or after the most special or important times, which really hurt and let me down. It's hard to accept that when you give someone so much love, time, and care that they could toss you out like an old shoe without thinking twice when you need them the most.

Now that I have recovered from these two toxic relationships, I am just so glad that both of these men are out of my life. I don't care who they are with or even how many times they cheated on me or lied to me. Once you advance in your recovery these details start to not matter. It really is a blessing not to have them around anymore. I like the person I am without them so much better than the person I was with them. I totally get that discard is traumatising and turns your whole world upside-down. If your partner turns other people against you in the process this makes it even more devastating. If you are recently experiencing this, hang in there - it does get better. Trust me, them leaving is a blessing in disguise. You'll see that soon.

REFLECTION POINTS

Can you think of a time when you were estranged or witnessed estrangement with a partner?

Have you experienced being discarded before? How did this make you feel?

When you are feeling out of control or something unexpected happens in your life, what helps to ground you?

Chapter 14

Third Time Lucky!

SO IF YOU ARE a repeat toxic relationship offender, like me, you may ask yourself, 'Will I ever get it right?' Will I ever finally see the red flags and get out before the craziness started up again? I think you will! No, I am not going to tell you a story about my new husband and twin boys, but I am going to tell you a very realistic recovery story. I would like to share an example that I am very proud of, in which I finally put what I'd learned into practice and didn't get sucked in by another narcissist. This was also kind of a mini psycho-social experiment for me to confirm my growth, recovery, and ability to identify and act on red flags.

Months after the dust settled from the breakup with Kyle, I went on a two-week getaway with some friends. My two friends are gay doctors and they really wanted to go to a gay-friendly beach town, so we did! It was summer in the UK so we headed to a small coastal town that has beautiful welcoming energy for the LGBTQ+ community; if you are straight, you are definitely in the minority there. For me, this was wonderful, as I was looking forward to spending time with friends and not having to worry about getting all dolled up to go out on the town. I thought I was the last person on the trip who would meet someone there because at first glance there seemed to be a significant shortage of straight men.

I always seem to meet narcissists in the strangest places; Miguel was my grandmother's doctor, Kyle knocked on my door to decorate, and Mark, well, he gave me a massage in the gay-friendly beach town! Now to be completely honest, my error has always been staying too long and not recognising the red flags early on. Well, I would like to share my story of Mark, and how this time I connected the dots and probably saved myself from another toxic relationship.

The first day of vacation my friends and I dragged our suitcases to our hotel. It was a fancy hotel and we decided to book some massages at the hotel spa. My two gay friends were excited about getting massages and casually commented about how they believed everyone who worked at the hotel was gay - I just assumed that they were right, and at that point, it was really unimportant information to me. When I saw my massage therapist, I thought to myself, 'lucky for the gay community, this is a gorgeous man.'

I enjoy chit chat and struggle to stay quiet long, so I started up a casual conversation with Mark during the massage. Mark told me that he usually kept to himself and didn't have a lot of friends in town. Since he was so handsome I quickly said to him that I was visiting with two gay friends and that he could hang out with us; undoubtedly one of my friends would like to meet this guy. Mark seemed to think this was a great idea. After the massage began, I started to question if this guy was gay; he told me he'd just got out of a 6-year relationship and had a two-year-old daughter. Then he started to tell me what pretty blue eyes I had.

Red flag: sharing a lot of information early on. This raised an alarm bell. Also, complementing a client's physical appearance - maybe not so appropriate?

To be honest, I would say it was the best massage I'd ever had; Mark was an excellent masseuse. Before my massage and meeting Mark, I had filled out a health information sheet with my address, phone number and allergies. I wasn't too surprised when 15 minutes after my massage, I got a text message from Mark saying how nice it was to meet me and that he hoped to see me soon. I wasn't surprised at all when he showed up at our hotel that night after his shift to hang out with my friends and me. I soon got the picture that he was not interested too much in my friends and was quite flirtatious and interested in me. Mark asked if I wanted to sit on the beach and talk or go back with him to his house.

My intuition quickly told me that this was a bad idea and I refused his invitation. I shared the location on my phone with my friends and told him we could chat alone in a public park, right next to the hotel downtown and where people passed by frequently. See - I was smart! I immediately picked up on his intense flattery and charm. For the first time, this registered right away!

Mark quickly told me how comfortable he was with me, how he felt that he didn't have to try with me and how he was convinced that I was going to fall in love with him in three days. Then came the compliments about how beautiful and exciting I was, and how he'd never met anyone like me before. Hmm - I remembered hearing these things a few times in the past... I thought to myself, 'I have only known Mark for less than three hours, he doesn't know me at all.' At this point, something was off; these compliments are not typical when first meeting someone.

Keep in mind Mark is probably the most physically attractive person by far who has ever shown interest in me; of course, the flattery was welcome, but I didn't fall for it. *It's nice when a handsome guy who is five years younger than you gives you a lot of attention, but this time I was mindful of the situation and that this over-the-top behaviour is something to be very suspicious of.* This was really the first guy I'd talked to in months after breaking up with Kyle, so the attention was nice, but I constantly told myself, 'don't get involved with this one.'

That night and the next day, I was flooded with text messages from Mark, asking when he could see me again. I felt like I was constantly bumping into Mark around the hotel too. I ran into Mark in the town before heading to dinner with my friends, and we sat on a bench and talked. He told me how crazy his ex was and what a relief it was to get away from her. Hmm, I think I'd heard that one before too. I also had a lot of 'crazy exes' stories to share, but I didn't - I am much more guarded with this information now.

Next Mark told me a hard to believe story about his family; hey, maybe it was true, but who knows? He told me how his mother had recently died; his sister had passed away due to being poisoned by her lesbian girlfriend and how he was estranged from his autistic father who lived in another part of the country. Hmmm… his family seemed to rival Kyle's stories about his crazy family. I responded to Mark with zero pity as he told his stories; I just nodded my head. Mark also told me he was kind of a "bad boy" and occasionally sold drugs. Who knows if any of this was true or not, but it was another big red flag. Remember, criminal activity and rule-breaking behaviours are right up the dysfunctional person's alley.

Keeping with the theme of honesty, I had to use a lot of self-talk and remind myself that there was something wrong with Mark. He was so attractive and looked like a model. Mark had swagger; he would look deep into my eyes, casually touch my hand, laugh at the right times, get close at the right times; basically, the guy had all of the right moves. He knew how to charm a lady. Each time I saw Mark over my vacation, I would tell my friends, "I am so proud I know this guy is a narcissist. He is hot as hell, but I know not to believe a word he says."

So needless to say, Mark started talking about coming to visit me at home, saying how he would be willing to move there to be with me. I thought this was absurd. What grown man says this after seeing me a few days in a row? The answer is a narcissist. I told him that it was a ridiculous idea. Even though overly passionate and extremely fast-moving, Mark was captivating to be around and had such presence. They all do! I won't lie and say I didn't enjoy spending time with him and that I didn't love all the attention of this cute guy. I just saw through his act.

Mark continued to text me after my vacation and eventually, I ended up blocking him. I stopped talking to him because I knew he had way too many red flags, to ever consider a friendship with him. *I knew his intentions were not pure, and that the odds to this ending badly were very high. I knew these things because I took the time to process my previous relationships and understand the patterns.* Even though I was coming out of another breakup, I was not vulnerable to this seductive man and his promises. I saw through his good looks, future-faking, flattery, attention, and stories. I knew when to get out and cut the ties when they needed to be cut.

So my advice to you is after you have healed and spent time being alone, it's okay to date. It's okay to get to know someone and have fun. It is also okay to break things off. If Mark lived in my hometown, I would have declined meeting him and blocked him immediately, but I was on vacation, and I wanted to test myself. It was good practice for me to set boundaries with a charming man, stop being a people-pleaser, and to be able to say no to things that made me feel uncomfortable.

Being honest, did I have a little fun with Mark? Yes. Did I know from the beginning it was only going to be holiday fun? Yes. Did I recognise and pay attention to red flags? Yes. Did I practice self-talk and pay attention to my intuition? Yes. I felt like this was the first legitimate evidence of my progress and emotional health. If I'd never taken the time to heal, process, and practice self-care, it would have been tempting to take Mark up on his offers. So that is the benefit of doing all the hard recovery work; you protect yourself the next time. Remember to celebrate small victories. Even though this was not a big life event, it made me feel like I was back on the right track. And hey, I got to have some fun with a handsome guy.

Even though I had fun, I was very smart about it. Smart as in, my friends at all times knew where I was when I was with Mark, and I met him in public places like the beach, in town, parks, and around the hotel. I didn't even get in his car with him or go to his house. Why so conservative, you may ask? Well, he did say he occasionally sold drugs, and I saw all those other red flags. I am fortunate that I have never been a victim of any type of physical abuse, but people with these traits can be dangerous. Whether you see red flags or not in your next dating adventure, it's okay to be cautious and take things slow.

It is also okay to date. Ever since Uni, I have been a serial monogamist. I go from one long-term relationship to the next, always staying a few extra years than I should have done. Serious relationships have always been my comfort zone. It's okay to step out of your comfort zone now and then; actually, I recommend it. If you have a type, give someone different a shot. Hey, you never know if vanilla is your favourite ice-cream flavour if you never try blueberry cheesecake crumble, right? So try other things! Be open-minded as you get back into dating.

I wish I'd dated more when I was younger. I also wish that change and life transitions didn't make me so anxious. It is usually very challenging to walk away from relationships, and no break-ups are fun. Life is short, so don't waste too much time on someone who isn't worth yours. You do not have to give anyone a second chance. When you feel like something isn't right, or someone hurts you, it is perfectly acceptable to walk away. I admit I am the queen of giving ninth and even tenth chances, and in the past, I stuck around in relationships for a few extra unnecessary years. This is something I am really working on, and so far I think I am doing rather well!

Red flags with Mark:

- Sharing too much of his personal life too soon
- Flirting on the job (boundaries)
- Overly sexual
- Superficial charm
- Extreme flattery
- Talking about his crazy ex
- Talking about illegal activities (selling drugs)
- Future-faking
- Fast-moving
- Lots of texts and calls right away

REFLECTION POINTS

- Have you started to date yet? Why or why not? What makes you feel ready to get close to someone again?
- Do you have a type? If so, what is it? Why is that your type?
- What are you open to in new relationships?
- Do you have any dating goals? What are they?

PART 5

"The secret to healing is when you learn that
YOU *had the power all along.....Be strong*
and fight for the future of drinking lemonade
in peace."

—TRACY A. MALONE

Chapter 15

Tools For Healing From Narcissistic Abuse

I WOULD LIKE TO take some time to share with you a few tools and techniques that I know work when healing from narcissistic abuse. These activities and ideas can be put into practice immediately and require nothing more than a little time and a journal or notebook. No matter how difficult or dysfunctional your relationship is or was with your toxic partner, whether you or they leave, or you are still in the relationship and figuring out how to leave, then these tools will give you the inner courage, and healing you need.

It is common to feel a whole host of emotions from anger, anxiety, confusion, sadness, fear, and shame at the end of a relationship. Your hormones and other chemicals in your body that bonded you to your narcissist also provoke strong emotional responses and pain. All of the ups and downs and the overall roller coaster ride makes ending a relationship with a narcissist so much more challenging than ending a healthy relationship.

I am going to give you some activities to support you as you recover. I also use these therapeutic interventions with my clients in my therapy sessions. You do not have to do all of these activities but find a few that you like and try them. I know recovery after narcissistic abuse is not easy, but you will heal and move on to bigger and better things!

Recovery is a process and that emotional pain you feel right now is one of the first signs of growth.

Feel your feelings; they serve a purpose! Please show yourself compassion and kindness during this process. Even if you acted crazy and did or said things that you regret, forgive yourself and show yourself, love.

If you feel scared, anxious, or stressed at home, talk to friends and identify three places where you can spend the night, pop in, or show up at any hour. Identify people who will always answer your call or your text. Knowing that you can reach out to others when you need a shoulder to cry on or a listening ear is very comforting. Let these people know that you are struggling and that you need them right now. Knowing that you have a safety net of at least three people who you can turn to when you need them will help you to feel supported, loved, and less anxious.

Positivity Exercises

One thing that we can always choose is our attitude. We can always decide how we are going to think about a situation and how we will respond. As we are recovering from narcissistic abuse, it is easy to feel down and negative thoughts can creep into our mind. These thoughts damage us and do not aid in our recovery. After a relationship with a narcissist, it is challenging to pick yourself up and see the good in people and the world.

This is normal and you have to make a conscious effort to have a positive attitude. Being positive will aid in your recovery. A positive attitude will lift your spirits and make you feel better. Like the other activities, this is something you need to practice.

Try some of the below suggestions if you find yourself thinking in negative ways.

A GRATITUDE JOURNAL

Write down five things that make you happy each day. You can then go back and see all the good things that happen to you daily when you are having a tough time. You do not need to name big or profound things but write down small daily pleasures like a good cup of tea, a phone call from your best friend, reading an interesting magazine article, recognising you got up on time and finding a good parking space downtown.

APPRECIATION

What we appreciate - appreciates!

Show your genuine appreciation to 5 people daily.

Sign off on emails, "With much appreciation."

By text or message, "I appreciate you".

With a smile on your face, "Much appreciated."

Pay attention to the reaction that you get and how appreciation makes you feel.

PRACTICE AFFIRMATIONS

When we affirm the positive traits that we have or would like to develop, we begin to focus on them - and whatever we focus on grows!

Affirmations are one way of doing this.

Create a series of statements starting with "I am…"

Here are a couple of examples:

"I am loved."

"I am loving."

"I am generous and kind."

"I am strong and resilient."

"I am worthy of love, kindness and compassion."

When you create your affirmations, set a reminder on your mobile or write them on a post-it and stick them up where you will see them every morning.

EXERCISE

Get out and move to release all of those feel-good chemicals in your body.

A brisk 20-minute walk daily will do wonders for your mental health. Any movement will do. Find an exercise that you enjoy so it will be easier for you to stick to it.

VOLUNTEER

Giving back is a great way to help your community, distract from your personal challenges and create a feeling of gratitude for what you have. Choose a charity or organisation that is close to your heart where you can add real value and feel motivated to help.

LEAN ON YOUR HIGHER POWER

Pray, go to church, meditate and explore your faith. Believing in something bigger than yourself will give you peace and make you more positive. It is also comforting and soothing. It doesn't matter if you believe in a religion, Karma, the universe - find some teachings that resonate with you. Having faith in something is very comforting during times of distress.

FORCE A SMILE

When you are feeling miserable or struggling with a situation, force yourself to smile. Smiling forces your body to release feel-good chemicals that give you a sense of light relief and positivity.

If you struggle to smile or forget, watch your favourite comedian on YouTube or Netflix or buy yourself a funny book. Laughter really is a great form of medicine!

FIND POSITIVE FRIENDS

Surround yourself with positive people who have a great outlook on life and consider the glass half-full. Good attitudes and positive perspectives rub off really easily when the people you turn to are always looking for the silver lining.

THE BIG CHOP!

It's time to remove the negative people from your life. Toxic relationships are not always romantic. If you have family members that bring you down, then create distance. If you have friends who complain, always have a negative response and look for ways to make things worse, then it's time to cut them loose. You're the sum of the 5 people closest to you in life - so choose carefully.

Mindfulness

If you have a therapist or read about mental health, I am sure by now you have heard the term "Mindfulness". There are so many books, workshops and YouTube channels that focus on the benefits of mindfulness and demonstrate the ways you can learn how to be mindful and practice mindfulness.

John Kabat Zinn is the pioneer and founding father of mindfulness as we know it today. He defined mindfulness as, "The awareness that arises from paying attention, on purpose, in the present moment and non-judgmentally." (Kabat-Zinn, in Purser, 2015).

I think it is also important to explain what mindfulness isn't.

Mindfulness is not a faith-based practice and is not a religion.

Mindfulness can be a form of meditation. Most major religions promote elements of mindfulness and meditation. You can be Christian, Jewish, Muslim, Buddhist, or Atheist and practice mindfulness. Think about mindfulness as an exercise for your brain, not your soul.

So what are the benefits of this mindfulness stuff? According to positivepsychology.com research has found that practising mindfulness can:

- Decrease stress and psychological distress
- Improve mental health
- Increase emotional regulation and self-control
- Decrease anxiety, depression, worry, and obsessive thoughts
- Reduce problem drinking behaviour
- Improve focus and attention
- Improve social and relational skills
- Reduce aggression
- Reduce symptoms of burnout
- Enhance job performance
- Improve resiliency

Now I am going to humbly give you my interpretation of mindfulness. To me, mindfulness is making a conscious effort to stay in and feel the current moment without bringing in information from the past or considering the possibilities that the future may bring.

Yes, this means making a conscious effort to not obsess and over-analyse your past relationship or worry about your next one. It means that if you feel sad to honour that sad feeling and not push it away or distract yourself from it.

Sometimes the current moment is positive or negative but being mindful is about observing deeply what is presently happening in your world without judging yourself or whatever is going on in your environment, as good or bad, positive or negative.

The life we modern humans live does not match how our brains were designed. Humans were never designed to stress about parking tickets, traffic, mortgage payments, and what we should do if we can't find a phone charger.

We certainly were not designed to dissect and figure out the ways and actions of a narcissist. We worry about what happened yesterday and what tomorrow may bring. Rarely are we engaged and attentive to what is actually happening right now.

The structure of our society breeds anxiety, stress, and insecurities. Sometimes the hardest thing to do when you are leaving a relationship and are stuck in your head with racing negative thoughts is to slow down and take a breath. It doesn't help that while you are recovering from narcissistic abuse you still have hundreds of other responsibilities that you have to juggle.

We all need to slow down and take a breath. Why not stop whatever you are doing, and take a deep breath right now!

That was nice, wasn't it?

So how can you practice mindfulness?

TEN BREATHS

Taking slow, deep breaths is one of my favourite mindfulness exercises and it works really well whether you are experienced or a complete beginner.

You are going to take ten long deep breaths in and breathe out fully and deeply on each exhale.

As you breathe in slowly and deeply through your nose and out again through your nose, see if you can pay attention to how your breath feels as it moves through your body.

Whenever you notice your thoughts distracting you, just acknowledge the thought as you would a passing neighbour in the street and return your focus to your breathing.

With your focus back to your breath, notice how it feels to breathe nice and deeply. Try to take ten deep breaths three times a day. Notice how you feel after you take those deep breaths.

You can also practice positive affirmations while you take in deep breaths.

Try saying the following statements to yourself with each of the breaths that you take:

- Breathe in… "I am healing" breathe out…
- Breathe in… "I deserve love" breathe out…
- Breathe in… "I deserve respect" breathe out…
- Breathe in… "I am beautiful" breathe out…
- Breathe in… "I am special" breathe out…
- Breathe in… "I am smart" breathe out…
- Breathe in… "I am worthy" breathe out…
- Breathe in… "I am calm" breathe out…
- Breathe in… "I am peaceful" breathe out…
- Breathe in… "I am a good person" breathe out…

THE SENSES

One of the recommendations that I give my clients who are starting out with mindfulness is, to begin with, the senses.

A great way of practising this is when you're out on a walk. So, the next time you are on a walk, pick a sense and pay attention to everything that surrounds you with this sense.

Let's try an example with hearing.

SOUND

Pay attention to all of the sounds that you hear - if any other thoughts come to mind, accept that they have shown up and then let go as you return to focusing on your hearing. You will notice that thoughts keep popping up in your mind and that's okay; just bring your focus back to the sounds in your environment.

SIGHT

Another idea is to observe something visually. Take a few moments to look at a flower on a picture, on a website or even in a vase.

Once you have found your flower, identify all of the colours and forms of the petals. How many different shades do you see? How would you describe that flower to someone? Only focus on the flower that you have chosen and when your mind starts to distract with thoughts of other things, thank it for sending you thought and return to noticing your flower.

TASTE

Mindful eating is another way to slow down your thoughts and focus on the present. Sometimes we eat so quickly and mindlessly, that we do not even taste what we are eating.

The next time you eat something, take the time to really taste your food.

For this exercise, let's pretend you are eating a strawberry. Before you take a bite, take a moment and look at the strawberry. What does it look like? How would you describe it?

Now take your fingers and gently touch the strawberry. What does it feel like? What words come to your mind?

Now smell the strawberry, how would you describe the smell? Fresh? Fruity? Now take a bite, notice the texture in your mouth, how does it feel?

Notice the taste now, what does it taste like? Sweet? Sour?

Now put the rest of the strawberry in your mouth and pay attention to how it sounds to chew the strawberry.

Eating mindfully in this way will help you to slow down, and really enjoy your food while practising being more mindful. This is a perfect example of an activity that helps you to take in the present moment and what you are doing. We have so many beautiful and inspirational moments to our days.

Unfortunately, we often miss special instances when we are recovering from narcissistic abuse. It is easy to get stuck in rumination and obsessive thought patterns.

Taking time to be present helps us to fully enjoy and recognise all the moments of our day. Even when you feel like your world is falling down and you have to drag yourself out of bed, there are still many positives in your life that are worth recognising.

Making an effort to be present and pay attention also is a way to take yourself out of the fog that so many survivors experience when they are recovering from narcissistic abuse.

Mindfulness is a very effective intervention if you tend to dissociate from your feelings too. Being mindful helps you to appreciate the little things in life. It also helps you to feel calm and at peace.

Being mindful helps us to slow down our mind and take control of the only thing we can, NOW. These activities also help you to leave the past where it belongs, in the past.

If you like these ideas I suggest you carry out an online search using the term mindfulness and you will certainly find plenty of new and exciting ways to become more mindful and enjoy all of the benefits I listed above.

Start small - maybe try to devote just 5 or 10 minutes to your mindfulness practise daily - and then slowly build it up to 30 - 60 minutes a day. If your mind wanders to your past relationship or what the narcissist will be doing in the future, just bring yourself back to the present moment and remember not to judge yourself or your thoughts.

Read & Write

READ - READ - READ

Read inspirational books.

Read memoirs.

Read self-help books.

Read about personality disorders and narcissistic abuse to educate yourself.

Read other survivors' stories.

Read books of poetry.

Read books of great heroes and heroines.

Reading is real therapy! Whatever you read fills you up. Reading is a great tool to help you through any negative or challenging situation. If you don't like reading then you can always listen - there are plenty of apps out there with audiobooks for you to listen to.

My favourite books in order:

1. In the Realm of Hungry Ghosts: Close Encounters with Addiction - By Gabor Maté

2. When the Body Says No: The Cost of Hidden Stress - By Gabor Maté

3. Psychopath Free - By Jackson MacKenzie

4. Buddha's Brain - The Practical Neuroscience of Happiness By Rick Hanson

5. To Kill a Mockingbird - By Harper Lee

6. Love in the Times of Cholera - Gabriela Garcia Marquez

7. A Dog's Purpose - By W. Bruce Cameron

8. It's Called a Breakup Because it's Broken: The Smart Girl's Break-Up Guide - By Greg Behrendt & Amiira Ruotola-Behrendt

WRITING

Writing can be extremely therapeutic as you recover from narcissistic abuse. Writing this book has brought me so much closure and has been such a healing experience for me.

Buy a journal and start writing down your thoughts and feelings. Below are some writing activity ideas that are very therapeutic. Try reading what you wrote aloud - this can be very powerful.

1. Write a letter to your childhood self. Tell her all of the things that you wish she knew. Comfort her. Write about your childhood wounds. Tell your younger self what is true and false about her beliefs.

2. Write down a list of all of the negative traits and behaviours of your ex that you managed to overcome. Rather like a list of achievements, it will help you to feel more confident and powerful - but will also remind you - on those weak moments, why you left! Pull out the list of all their bad traits when you have an urge to contact them.

3. Write a letter to your ex-partner. This can be a tough one. In time, when you feel stronger, sit down and write a letter to the narcissist in your life. Tell them the things you wish they knew, and anything that you really need to get off of your chest. This is not a letter to send to them - it's an opportunity

for you to express all of the pain they have caused you, and also works as a tool for closure. When you are done you can rip it up or burn it.

Epilogue

WHEN A RELATIONSHIP ENDS, it is never easy. Even if a relationship ends well, there is grieving that needs to be done. *When a relationship with a narcissist or toxic individual ends, it's ten times worse. It takes a lot of work, courage, time, and dedication to begin healing yourself.* It is a doable journey but not quick, and most of it starts by going uphill. The good thing is that there are so many interventions, therapies, and supports out there to aid you on your way to healing.

If the wound is fresh, I get how overwhelming starting this journey is. If this is your second major wound from a toxic relationship, I know that it is even tougher to start your recovery. Healing is a process, but it is well worth the time that you invest in it. *You can and will get yourself back together and have a wonderful life. You can and will feel happy, safe, and calm again. Each day it gets better, little by little.*

The advice, tips and examples in this book all come from my personal experiences and training in the mental health field. I do not consider myself an expert on personality disorders. Still, I do feel like my mental health background, and two experiences with covert and overt toxic partners, give me a unique perspective on the subject matter. I hope my story and journey has helped you and made you feel supported and not alone.

If you do a quick google search, you will see there is a strong community of survivors of narcissistic abuse. There are countless forums, blogs, web pages and books dedicated to the subject matter. Be an educated consumer of research and try to find adequate resources to guide you. Keep in mind that not everything that you see on the internet is good advice and that anyone can make a webpage. Look for information from mental health professionals. Be careful not to get stuck on forums that are just complaining stations. Try to find options that focus on healing you and supporting your emotional wellbeing.

I also strongly encourage you to find a good therapist. *Your first therapist doesn't have to be your "forever therapist". It is okay to switch therapists or shop around until you find a good fit.* You may want to ask if they have experience working with survivors of narcissistic abuse or about their training in personality disorders. *Talk to your therapist about doing some family of origin work. I strongly recommend analysing your childhood and your relationship with your caregivers to obtain more insight into your adult relationships.*

This was a difficult thing for me to do. I love my parents so much, and I know they love me even more than I love them. I fully believe that they tried to do the best that they could given the resources that were available to them when I was growing up. Parents aren't perfect, and parenting is a tough job.

Even though in this book I point to patterns of behaviours and lessons I learned as a child leading me to problems in my adult relationships, my parents did many good things during my childhood and were always supportive and continue to be. I also learned great values and lessons from my mum and dad. When you analyse your childhood, try to dedicate time to the positive and the negative. Understand that the same event or parenting style impacts every child differently and what you took out of childhood will probably be different than what your siblings, who were living in the same house, internalised. Events and people impact us all differently, and sometimes little things lead to big problems, and big things lead to less damage than one would anticipate. That is just the serendipity of life.

Returning to the recovery from your romantic relationship, *everyone recovers from narcissistic abuse in a different way. There is no one-size-fits-all remedy.* I think if you want to focus on healing, a combination approach is a good idea. After Miguel, I was so busy with work and starting a second master's degree that biweekly therapy sessions and distraction tactics were my recovery plan. Looking back, this wasn't enough, and I should have focused more energy on healing. Instead of feeling and processing the pain, I tried to pretend that everything was fine when inside I was hurting. Recognise and feel your feelings, or they will come up later and maybe even harder to deal with then.

I made a lot of errors during recovery from my relationship with Miguel. I was so used to jumping at Miguel's beck and call that it was tough to go no contact. I convinced myself that there were legitimate reasons to still talk to him when there really weren't any. Sadly, I think I was afraid to stop talking to him. It was hard to break old habits. How was I not furious that the guy I was living with impregnated another woman and was lying and cheating? I think this goes back to childhood patterns of being taught that in my house it wasn't acceptable for me to be angry. I also think subconsciously when my parents or anyone else would be mad at me I would freeze and dissociate from my feelings, so I practised doing this too. I also didn't like how angry people made me feel, and I did not want to be an angry person. Now I get that anger can be a healthy emotion and we should express it appropriately.

Once I did finally stop talking to Miguel, my healing process sped up. *I understand that when someone is very controlling, and you are used to walking on eggshells to avoid problems, breaking off contact can seem impossible and even scary.* In my own way, talking to Miguel even made me feel like I had some kind of control that he would not show up on my doorstep or become angrier. Remember you can only control yourself, and the last person you are ever going to control or influence is your toxic ex-partner. Start no contact as soon as you can. After a while, it gets easier.

Moving on to Kyle, a mistake I made was giving him so many chances and not going no contact sooner. I can tell you the first time I should have broken things off with Kyle, but I gave him a second chance, then a third, then a fourth, then a fifth. I didn't want to go through another breakup. I wanted so badly to believe that Kyle was a "good guy" and "the one" that I missed the subtle ways he wasn't treating me well, like every so often trying to break up with me because he wasn't good enough or had a mental health breakdown right before a big event or holiday.

The first time he did this, I should have said goodbye and good luck. After finding out about all the affairs, it was effortless to go no contact and stick to it. If you haven't started 'no contact,' today is as good as any day to begin! It is okay to have high standards and hold people accountable for bad behaviour.

In my experiences with both Miguel and Kyle, rumination and staying stuck in my head were significant roadblocks to recovery. Don't get me wrong, talking about your pain and processing your feelings is vital to recovery, but there is a right and wrong way to process. The rumination happens because of the cycle of love-bombing, idealisation, devaluing and then discarding. This process creates and reinforces the trauma bond, mainly because it tends to be a cycle and happens over and over again. Feeling confusion and cognitive dissonance is natural, and anyone would want to figure out what happened and why.

My suggestion is to tell your story, vent to friends and family but don't waste your valuable energy and time trying to figure out the "whys" of your narcissist. Often we think if we know why then we can fix the behaviour. *Narcissists rarely change, and it is not our job to fix them.* Try telling yourself this situation is crazy, and crazy does not make sense. *I am guilty of trying to be a detective too and going over scenarios and possible explanations of their behaviours in my head for hours. That did not help me to feel better or give me any answers. Analysing and trying to figure out why - did not change anything!* Looking back I wish I would have used that time I spent ruminating, focusing on healing instead.

I know this is easier said than done. *When a relationship ends or something unexpected happens it's difficult to think or talk about anything else. So what can you do? This is where I would suggest practising mindfulness.* I advise trying meditation or working on breathing for a few minutes when you catch yourself in a rumination rut. If you can change your environment that is often extremely helpful. Go outside or to a different room, go for a walk or just stand up if you are sitting. Sometimes a physical change can help support a change in thinking. You can try to set a time of day when you are going to think about the relationship and make a commitment to only ruminate for a set time limit. Practising self-care and doing something that you enjoy is another strategy that you can use when you find yourself stuck obsessing about the relationship. Make a list of all the little things that bring you joy or activities that can help you break the rumination cycle so you can pull it out when you are stuck in a rut.

After my relationship with Kyle ended I knew I needed to do more than my previous recovery plan of therapy every two weeks and distract myself. *This time I really tried to tackle my recovery like a psychologist would. I asked myself what kind of treatment plan and advice would I give someone in my situation? How can I use my knowledge about mental health, trauma, anxiety and depression to help myself?* Adopting this philosophy helped me to make much better choices during my recovery from Kyle. This time I really pushed myself to get better and focus on healing.

I promised myself I would not date or look for a relationship and I stuck to it. I knew I needed to learn how to be alone and happy with myself first. This at times was very hard. I was proud of myself for not wanting to find another man to fill the void Kyle left. *I did feel lonely and sad at times but I knew I had to sit in the emotions in order to heal and be ready for a relationship one day.* When I would feel lonely I would use compassionate self-talk and try to guide myself through that rough patch. *I found that naming and writing down my emotions and why I thought I was feeling them was very helpful. I would also tell myself that these feelings were normal and I welcomed them instead of trying to push them aside.*

For example, I would wake up in the morning feeling anxious. When I felt that nervous feeling in my chest and stomach I would put my hands over those parts of my body and say, "I am feeling anxious because I am scared and getting used to being alone. I am going to care for myself and show myself understanding, I will be okay." Positive self-talk is very important during your recovery. *Don't be afraid to identify your feelings and comfort yourself.* This can be very soothing and help with healing. I would suggest every few hours taking a five-minute break to think about how you are feeling and comfort yourself if you are struggling.

In addition to self-talk and working on self-compassion, I increased my therapy to weekly sessions. I had my therapist who I have worked with for years and then I started to do Eye Movement Desensitisation and Reprocessing (EMDR) work to process trauma caused by these relationships with another therapist. In my experience the combination of talk therapy and trauma-focused therapy was helpful. My "forever therapist" uses cognitive behaviour therapy techniques during sessions which involve homework. I took these assignments seriously.

Counsellors are great resources and so are friends but I didn't limit my support system to just loved ones and therapists. I also talked to psychics, priests, spiritual advisors, and people I didn't even know on narcissistic abuse forums. I was open to exploring a multitude of avenues to feel better. Everyone has a different perspective on these kinds of relationships and healing. Take the advice that makes sense to you and that is helpful. Disregard the other information. Make sure you stay focused on processing your feelings and make the conversations about you. *Analysing or asking all those "why" questions about them won't help too much with your healing.* If you get stuck in a rumination cycle, and I have been there and I know it is easy to do, tell yourself, "He/she is mentally ill and that is why he/she did this. I need to focus on me and what will make me feel better."

So the question then becomes how do you focus on you and what to do to feel better? This is different for everyone. I have never enjoyed exercise but I know the research behind it and getting your heart rate up releases lots of feel-good chemicals. I made an effort to do at least twenty minutes of exercise a day. I also did yoga and ballet which was like medicine for my mind and body. I practised mindfulness while walking my dog and tried to be out in nature as much as I could. Personally working on deep breathing and staying present in nature was soothing for me. I started my recovery from Kyle during late spring so the temperature was perfect to be outside and active.

I also journaled during my recovery from Kyle. Knowing that I never completely processed and recovered emotionally from Miguel, I journaled about that experience as well. I also journaled about my childhood wounds. Sometimes I would look in the mirror and read what I wrote out loud. Sometimes I would read what I wrote to my therapist and friends. If you are not sure what to write about, start by writing a letter letting your partner know how he/she hurt you and how you feel. These letters are not to be delivered, so you can be honest. Try writing a letter to your childhood self and let him/her know how sorry you are about your wounds and pain. You can write a letter to your future self as well as anticipating all the good things that recovery will bring.

In addition to journaling about the relationship, write about you. Write about the traits that you admire and what you want to change about yourself. Make a list of things that you need to forgive yourself for. *Abuse is never your fault* and is always wrong. Still, as survivors, we need to recognise that we could have made different or better decisions to protect ourselves during the relationship. We cannot change the past, but we certainly can learn from it and apply what we learned in the future.

So to sum up this whole story, I would like to conclude by saying thank you, my reader, for also being part of my healing journey. Writing this book has been very therapeutic for me and has helped to provide more closure to my two toxic relationships. I genuinely hope that my stories and my tips will be useful to you in your recovery. I know how painful and tough it is to be in and leave a relationship with a narcissist. It really turns your whole life upside-down, but it doesn't have to stay that way. You can take steps to recover and find peace and happiness. Take the time to learn who you are and really discover your story starting with your childhood. Focus on the "why" questions about your behaviour and thinking to get insight. Take care of yourself and work hard to get better, I know you can! My hope for you is that you will learn from and reflect on your toxic relationship and your past and be able to let go of all the pain, trauma and hurt. I wish you happiness, love, and peace.

Author Bio

JENNY HAS WORKED IN mental health for over 12 years providing outpatient counselling, workshops, and conducting diagnostic testing and evaluations. Professionally her interests include mindfulness, childhood psychological disorders, learning disabilities, addictions, and anxiety. In therapy sessions, Jenny uses an eclectic mix of cognitive behavioural therapy techniques, visualisation strategies, meditation techniques, and breath work to help her clients achieve their goals. Jenny also has a master's degree in French and loves to travel and explore new cultures and countries. In her free time, Jenny enjoys spending time with her family and friends but what she loves most is being outside in nature with her dog. She is starting to explore the world of writing and is truly enjoying this new professional endeavour.

Notes

I thought it would be great for you to keep all of your notes in one place. The following pages are laid out for you to make notes, write your reflections and some of the exercises in the Healing section.